THE REUNIFICATION OF

GERMANY

edited by ROBERT EMMET LONG

THE REFERENCE SHELF

Volume 64, Number 1

THE H. W. WILSON COMPANY

New York   1992

THE REFERENCE SHELF

The books in this series contain reprints of articles, excerpts from books, and addresses on current issues and social trends in the United States and other countries. There are six separately bound numbers in each volume, all of which are generally published in the same calendar year. One number is a collection of recent speeches; each of the others is devoted to a single subject and gives background information and discussion from various points of view, concluding with a comprehensive bibliography that contains books and pamphlets and abstracts of additional articles on the subject. Books in the series may be purchased individually or on subscription.

Library of Congress Cataloging-in-Publication Data

The reunification of Germany / edited by Robert Emmet Long.
    p.   cm. — (The Reference shelf ; v. 64. no. 1)
    Includes bibliographical references.
    ISBN 0-8242-0825-0
    1. Germany—History—Unification, 1990.   2. Germany—History—1990-   I. Long, Robert Emmet.   II. Series.
DD262.R48   1992
943.087′9—dc20   91-43545
                                                             CIP

Cover: "Peace Unites Europe and Germany"—reads the poster carried by demonstrators that assembled at East Berlin's Alexander Square.
Photo: AP/Wide World Photos

Printed in the United States of America

CONTENTS

PREFACE

The winding down of the Cold War and the tumultuous changes taking place within the Soviet Union and its neighboring countries in eastern Europe stand out dramatically as the most significant events of recent times. Political upheaval in Europe has been particularly momentous in Germany, where the most unpredictable events have occurred with breath-taking suddenness, and with implications that have not yet been fully measured. For four decades the German Democratic Republic (GDR) in the East and the Federal Republic of Germany (FRG) in the West were divided physically as well as symbolically by the Berlin Wall, and a union between the two could hardly have been forseen in our time. Even in 1988, when West German Chancellor Helmut Kohl was asked, "Will you yourself experience unification?" he replied, "No, probably I will not live to see it." Yet within a year the Berlin Wall was opened, and on October 3, 1990 unification formally occurred. On December 2, 1990, Kohl, an advocate of unification, was elected chancellor of the new, united Germany, the capital of which will move from Bonn to Berlin.

This compilation assesses the extraordinary events in Germany in the last several years. It begins with a section that contrasts East and West Germany. The differences between them, as the articles in this section make clear, are stark and dramatic. While West Germany enjoys the highest standard of living in Europe, East Germany has been plunged into uncertainty and depression in its painful attempt to convert from a Soviet-style to a free market economy. Section Two considers the phenomenon of mass immigration into West Germany not only by East Germans but also by ethnic Germans living formerly in the Soviet Union and such eastern European countries as Yugoslavia, Romania, Hungary, and Czechoslovakia. Section Three examines the fall of the old regime in the GDR, particularly the dissolution of its army and its secret police establishment (commonly called Stasi), a mammoth surveillance and spy network. Section Four contains articles that raise the question of whether a Germany unified for the first time since the defeat of Hitler can be trusted in the years ahead. The articles also discuss the country's future relations to the United States, the Soviet Union, NATO, and the European community.

The editor is indebted to the authors and publishers who have granted permission to reprint the materials in this compilation. Special thanks are due Joyce Cook and the Fulton Public Library staff, and the staff of Penfield Library, State University of New York at Oswego.

ROBERT EMMET LONG

September 1991

I. AFFLUENT WEST GERMANY/COLLAPSED EAST GERMANY

EDITOR'S INTRODUCTION

The contrast presented by the eastern and western parts of Germany today is startling. West Germany possesses one of the world's most dynamic economies and enjoys a prosperity that is the envy of Europe, while East Germany is in a state of demoralization and economic collapse. East Germany, of course, has long been overshadowed by its western neighbor. The Berlin Wall was erected precisely to stem the exodus of thousands of citizens in the East in search of a higher living standard and political freedom in the West. But with the opening of the Wall, East Germany's Communist political structure was not only strained but actually disintegrated. Its people now face the daunting task of converting from a command economy to a market economy. As businesses continue to fail, unemployment is expected to rise to record levels. A mood of disillusionment now grips East Germany, even though in the long run, with new investment, the region is expected to recover.

The first article, by William Rademaekers in *Time*, discusses West Germany's "economic miracle" that has given its people the best wages in Europe for the shortest work week and enabled them to travel abroad in large numbers. It can boast both of success in the work place and a lifestyle of leisure.

The next article, by John Marks writing in *U.S. News & World Report*, estimates that Germany will need $1.2 trillion over the next decade to rejuvenate the deteriorated economy of the eastern region. Marks also points out that one institution, the Treuhand, or government privitization agency, has been assigned to rehabilitate and sell off to private interests as many of the former state-owned enterprises as possible. In "Why Don't They Shave," reprinted from *Newsweek*, Charles Lane discusses the political backlash that Chancellor Helmut Kohl is encountering as estimates of the cost of reunification and the taxes to pay for it escalate.

Another aspect of East Germany's situation, dealt with by

Michael Mayer in a *Newsweek* article, is pollution and environmental destruction. After forty years of communism, environmental damage in the east is widespread and the cleanup cost will be astronomical. Two concluding articles sound more hopeful notes. In a piece from *Fortune,* Shawn Tully describes the climate for foreign investment in eastern Germany and the entrepreneurial opportunities it offers. In the final article, reprinted from *Forbes,* Jerry Flint focuses on the automobile industry in East Germany. The Trabant is an inefficiently-produced car of low-grade quality, an apt symbol of the failed East German economic system. However, foreign automakers expect to take advantage of a competent, mechanically adept work force and restructure the industry. Flint predicts boom times ahead.

THE OH SO GOOD LIFE[1]

An old German description of well-being is to live *wie Gott in Frankreich*—like God in France. Whatever the yardstick for the good life, at least some of it still seems to be outside Germany. In pursuit of that grail, some 800,000 West Germans have established second homes abroad—in Tuscany, along the Grande Corniche overlooking the Riviera, in the verdant valleys of South Tirol. They have also become the world's most traveled tourists: last year some 28 million West Germans took holidays abroad.

East Germans have a great deal of catching up to do, but they are trying. Hardly was the Wall down when a trickle of East Berliners and Leipzigers and Dresdeners appeared on the Champs Elysées and the Via Veneto. Long confined to holidays within the socialist bloc—beaches on the Black Sea or the chilly waters of the Baltic—thousands of Easterners will no doubt soon set out for venues of the *dolce vita,* the requisite deutsche marks in their pockets.

For West Germans, the annual migrations have had a profound impact on taste and spending habits. Looking at the shops in urban centers, a visitor might think himself in the wrong coun-

[1]Article by William Rademaekers, staffwriter, from *Time* 136:80–82 Jl 9'90. Copyright 1990 The Time Inc. Magazine Company. Reprinted by permission.

try. Here a Benetton, there a Chloë, a Chanel, farther along a Giorgio Armani, a Fendi, a Valentino. The name of every other restaurant seems to begin with *le* or *la*, and every other menu includes a dish or two from faraway places. Better off than ever before, West Germans are spending fortunes to keep up with the Schmidts; money appears to be no object in the pursuit of distinctive art or eye-catching design in clothes, cars, houses, even the simplest household objects. A society long praised—and sometimes derided—for an overgrown work ethic has turned its restless energies to the cultivation of leisure. Enveloped in superlatives, West Germany has emerged as one of the world's most affluent societies: the nation with the largest trade surplus; the greatest per capita concentration of high-performance automobiles; the best wages for the shortest work week; and the most rewarding all-round standard of living among major industrialized countries.

"Never in our history have we lived so well," says former Economics Minister Count Otto Lambsdorff. Statistics bear him out. In the past three decades the supply of goods and services has quintupled and consumption quadrupled. The living standard since the '50s has improved at an annual rate of 4%. Net monthly income has expanded tenfold in that period, hourly wages almost eightfold. In the early '60s, the average family spent half its income on food and household goods; today the figure is slightly over 20%. Nearly as much——15%—is devoted to leisure activities and holidays.

At least 400 families control fortunes in excess of $100 million, but the real measure of wealth lies in its breadth and depth. More than 2 million people, many only in their 30s, are deutsche mark millionaires. This is the first German generation in this century to actually inherit wealth. "Earlier generations," says Edith Hartl, a self-made businesswoman in Munich, "were wiped out by Weimar inflation or war. Today's 30-year-olds are inheriting all the fruits of the economic miracle."

They have no qualms about spending the inheritance. Sabena Knust, owner of a Munich art gallery, says lots of money is being poured into modern art: an original painting by a contemporary artist goes for $50,000, a print for $4,000. Regina Spelman, an editor at the German-language *Harper's Bazaar,* sees vast amounts being spent on apparel: "Germans use clothes to define their place in society and are willing to spend a lot to make a statement." Hamburg Designer Peter Schmidt notes that "people are

willing to pay to surround themselves with well-designed things."
Kurt Gustmann, an editor at the magazine *Schöner Wohnen* in
Hamburg, points to a general pattern of cultivating leisure ac-
tivities based on long weekends.

Anna Golin, who owns Wunderhaus, a giant warehouse of
modern furnishings in Unterföhring, says people are investing
heavily in home decoration as well: a Rolf Sachs chair goes for
$5,900, a chest of drawers by Shiro Kuramata for $8,900. The
furniture fills high-priced housing. A no-frills single-family house
in choice areas of Baden-Württemberg or Bavaria averages about
$300,000, a one-bedroom apartment rarely less than $160,000.
The most reasonably priced region is along the East-West border,
but even there the market is tight.

The key word in the great pursuit of pleasure is *Luxus*, or
luxury. It is commonly used these days to describe ashtrays,
bathrooms, cars, furnishings, graphics, holidays—just about anything used in everyday life that is well-designed or distinctive.
Frequently it means something outrageously expensive. G&M, a
mail-order house in Bavaria, caters specifically to such tastes, offering a catalog of 273 "carefully selected luxury gifts," with a
total value of $26.5 million; among them are a Tabriz rug for
$964,000 and a gold-plated record player for $75,000. Dieter
Schiwietz, a Hamburg plastic surgeon, says women—and men—
seem to be having no trouble finding money for face-lifts costing
up to $70,000. Says Schiwietz: "Looking good is an important
part of the good life."

The outpouring of wealth has been accompanied by a remarkable transformation in the work ethic. According to a survey by
the Allensbach Institute, modern Germany "has changed from a
working society to a leisure society." The average person, it notes,
devotes four hours a day to leisure activities, in contrast to about
1½ hours 40 years ago. That comes as no surprise to anyone who
has attempted to reach a government official in Bonn after 3 p.m.
Much of the country, in fact, seems to operate on a distinctly non-
Teutonic mañana principle. *Freizeit*, or leisure time, is sacred, and
work is, at best, a distraction.

The Latinization of Germany can be seen in lingering lunch
breaks, overflowing cafés, empty offices, on packed golf courses
or deserted city streets on weekends. "The Germans," complains
one employer, "have more short breaks and holidays than anyone

else." Adding it all up, the average West German has at least two months off a year.

Yet, magically, although they work less, they manage to produce more and still maintain quality. That is due partly to their guest workers, who get their hands dirty running many of the production lines, partly to a genius for organization and supervision.

The cornucopia of wealth and well-being has brought some strange insecurities. "*Luxus* is a way of trying to making yourself different from others," complains Munich socialite Heidi Schoeller, the wife of a banker. "Money doesn't mean very much in a society where everyone has it."

There is a near manic devotion to *Trendforschung*, or trend research, to discover what is In or Out. The newest trend in holidays, for instance, is to avoid other Germans—even if that means spending a month in Patagonia. The drift in sports is to golf; tennis has become "too popular" since Boris Becker first took the Wimbledon crown in 1985. Although the waiting period in Germany for Mercedes-Benz's latest sports car, the $77,000 500SL, is four years, the trendy automobile is something like an Isdera Imperator, built by a small company in Stuttgart, which uses a Mercedes-Benz V-8 engine but certainly does not look like a Mercedes-Benz.

No one has yet gauged the potential impact of the great disparity between ostentatious affluence in the West and relative poverty in the East, but that is a grating issue and not likely to disappear soon. Perhaps aware of this, along with the realization that life may have become too lavish, a few West Germans are tuning in to something called *Neue Bescheidenheit,* or new modesty—an effort to get back to the essentials of the good life. It has had only modest success. "This is like Jackie Kennedy's basic black and pearls," says one critic. "The pearls are genuine, the basic black is cashmere, and the accessories are Hermès or Vuitton."

Other, equally ambitious—and more than likely passing— trends are on the horizon. "The newest form of chic," says Hartl, "is to learn things other people don't know—to actually read a book, for instance." That may also be short-lived because as good as it is, contemporary German life is hardly restful or contemplative. "We're still trying to define ourselves," says Schmidt.

"Even in leisure we're not particularly at ease." God, in other words, has not moved to Germany. Not yet.

THE COST OF GERMAN UNITY[2]

Helmut Kohl wasn't on hand in Leipzig last week, but every time the German chancellor's name was mentioned at a mass demonstration, a throng of 60,000 angry people booed and hissed. Some members of the hostile eastern German crowd carried banners reading "liar" and "pig." The animosity toward Kohl was striking: A little more than a year ago, the German leader was applauded by 100,000 citizens in the same town square while campaigning on a platform of national unity and pro-business prosperity.

The cheers have turned to jeers because Kohl has thus far failed to deliver on his enticing promises. There's no question that liberating East Germany from the Communists enhanced Western security. But in the six months since reunification, the economy of the eastern part of the country has virtually collapsed. Industrial output has been halved as thousands of companies— from shipbuilders to sweet shops—have proved incapable of surviving against Western competition. And nearly 800,000 eastern Germans are currently unemployed, while an additional 1.8 million people are working shortened hours in a labor force of just under 8 million. By the end of 1991, according to some estimates, more than half of all eastern Germans will be unemployed and only 20 percent of the businesses from the old Communist regime will be operating. To reverse this deterioration, analysts believe that nearly $1.2 trillion will be needed over the next decade to rejuvenate eastern Germany.

The crisis facing Kohl stems largely from 45 years of Communist neglect and decay. Once the wall between the two Germanys was ripped down, it became clear that the industrial sector in the east was weaker than anticipated. When they visited once impris-

[2]Article by John Marks and Robert F. Black, staff writers, from *U.S. News & World Report* 110:48–50 Ap 1 '91. Copyright Anril 1, 1991 *U.S. News & World Report.* Reprinted by permission.

oned cities like Dresden and Leipzig, western officials found antiquated factories and a work force that couldn't produce for the global marketplace. "We deceived ourselves about the ability of businesses in eastern Germany to survive," confessed Kohl during a recent TV appearance.

Poor planning. Kohl also may have misled the German public last year, when he pushed through a rapid monetary union between eastern and western Germany that included an overly generous exchange rate. Despite warnings from his central bank that swapping East Germany's worthless money for the powerful West German mark on a 1-to-1 basis would be inflationary, the chancellor persevered in order to foster unity, a politically popular goal.

The dire predictions have come true, as long deprived easterners have gone on spending sprees for Western goods, further undermining their own local economy. Last week, the president of Germany's central bank, Karl Otto Pöhl, blasted Kohl's expediency. "The result is disaster, as we can see," Pöhl said. Eastern Germany is now "completely uncompetitive."

Unification has boomeranged on western Germany, too. In the process of integrating its eastern neighbor over the past few months, the world's third-largest economy has suffered one humiliating setback after another. For starters, the surge in consumer spending has begun to drive up prices. German inflation last year stood at 2.7 percent, but it is expected to reach 3.5 percent before the year is out. Increased consumer demand in the east has also sucked in huge amounts of imported goods. As a result, Germany, once the world's largest exporter, recently posted its first monthly current-account deficit since August 1985. In January, the nation turned in a current-account shortfall of $800 million, a sharp turnaround from the $6.8 billion surplus it chalked up a year earlier. And while Germany may not have a permanent trade deficit, its surplus is expected to shrink over the next year.

Germany's economic growth is now dragging even more than initially anticipated as a result of unification. The government recently reduced its estimated increase for gross national product to between 2.5 percent and 3 percent, down from more than 3 percent. This represents a significant drop-off from West Germany's GNP jump of 4.6 percent last year.

Growth will be further retarded by the recent tax hike that the financially strapped and overcommitted Kohl government was forced to implement. By boosting personal income taxes and most consumer taxes, the chancellor hopes to raise an additional

$10.8 billion this year and $17 billion in the first half of 1992. These funds will help pay for the massive rebuilding of the east as well as Germany's $11.4 billion contribution to the gulf war effort and nearly $9.1 billion in outstanding loans to the Soviet Union that must be written off.

Towering rates. Germany has also had to borrow heavily in the bond markets. This dependence has pushed domestic long-term interest rates over 9 percent—bad news for most of Europe's slowing economies. Because the deutsche mark is the anchor currency for Europe, countries on the Continent are forced to maintain interest rates at the German level in order to keep their currencies strong and attract needed capital. High interest rates are particularly painful for a recessionbound country like France, which is expected to grow at less than 2 percent this year and needs to slash interest rates to stimulate its dormant economy. Last week, the Bank of France cut its short-term lending rates, but it was constrained by Germany's toweringly high rates and could only shave off a meager quarter point.

German unification could similarly hamstring the struggling American economy by forcing the Federal Reserve to keep U.S. rates competitive with Germany's. This could dilute and delay a strong economic recovery in this country. In addition, high interest rates that further slow European economies mean that U.S. exports, a major source of growth, could suffer.

As damaging as the U.S. recession has been domestically, it is far less punitive than the economic plague that currently grips eastern Germany. In the six months since German unification, highways, sewers and polluted water supplies have not been improved. Street lights have been switched off. Telephones still do not work. Services like child care and sanitation pickup have disappeared. Hospitals and libraries have closed. To make matters worse, in August major rent increases will be heaped upon millions of residents in low-cost housing units for the first time. And bankrupt city and state governments don't have the resources to fight the escalating disintegration.

Dark thoughts. The bleak economic future has clearly destroyed the confidence of eastern Germans and made them deeply pessimistic. In a poll taken a year ago by a German business magazine, 35 percent of the plant managers in eastern Germany expressed despair about the future. When the same poll was taken in January, the number of doom-and-gloomers had risen to 85 percent. In the northern city of Schwerin, the gatekeeper at a plastics machinery plant sips coffee and echoes his countrymen. "We're all going to end up in the streets," he says. "My son has lost his job, but my wife still naively believes things will get better. Not me. I dream of going to Canada, where there's plenty of space and fewer people."

One institution, the Treuhand, or government privatization agency, has been assigned to rehabilitate as many of the former state owned enterprises as possible. The companies are then to be sold off. With 8,000 businesses and a payroll of 3.9 million people, the Treuhand is the largest and most diversified holding company in the world, and its decisions have already affected nearly everyone in eastern Germany.

So far, 1,000 of the 8,000 businesses in the Treuhand's custody have been sold, according to a member of the agency's board. Radio Television of Thuringia, an entertainment electronics company, for example, secured an investment from a western German telecommunications firm before flying off from the Treuhand's protective nest. "We never waited for the Treuhand to come to us," said Gert-Rudiger Merkert, director of Radio Television. "We activated ourselves. We were always there, saying 'We want to do this, we want to do that.'"

Wartburg, a maker of automobiles, wasn't as lucky. The Treuhand shut down the car maker in late January, sentencing more than 10,000 workers to a long period of unemployment. Subsidizing the plant would have cost $121.8 million, said a Treuhand spokesman. Instead, the money will be used to fund training and unemployment programs for workers. The Treuhand has come under fire from protesters, who say that the agency is often too quick to shut down a company rather than reinvigorate it and sell it. "End this policy of the Treuhand," roared Jochen Kletzin, a union leader attending the Leipzig demonstration last week. "We want to preserve our jobs!"

Unemployment in eastern Germany may taper off if investors from the West can be lured into the battered region. Coca-Cola, one of the first to take a giant step forward, plans to spend $274 million to open up a distribution network in the east. And in 1992, Opel and Mercedes will establish plants in the southeastern city of Eisenach, one of the worst hit areas in the country. Rebuilding eastern Germany will require huge amounts of time, money and patience. But the onerous process must begin in earnest or restive crowds around the country could eventually drive Helmut Kohl, "the great unifier," and his government from office.

'WHY DON'T THEY SHARE?'[3]

Just four months ago, Helmut Kohl was the toast of Leipzig. Hundreds of thousands of flag-waving Germans filled the university town's Karl Marx Platz to hail the man who promised to rescue them from socialism's failures. "Helmut, Helmut!" chanted the Leipzigers. Last week they had a new name for their leader. Seventy thousand angry people filled the same plaza to condemn the man who promised that "nobody will lose" from German unification. "Liar!" they shouted. "Pig!"

Helmut Kohl is encountering a political backlash. With eastern Germany's economy in a state of near collapse, nearly three quarters of the region's people say they are "disappointed" with him. Half of all western Germans agree. All Germans will soon shoulder heavy new taxes to pay for reunification—a tax Kohl promised never to impose. Disgruntlement with the chancellor reigns in Western capitals, too, thanks to the German government's lukewarm embrace of allied effort in the Persian Gulf War. The heady emotions of reunification that carried Kohl to a third term last December have given way to the hard task of welding two unequal societies into a single nation capable of a constructive global role. And many Germans are wondering if their chancellor is up to the job. "Somehow Kohl doesn't look anymore like the figure who can supervise unification in all of its enormous philosophical, mental and psychological dimensions," says Meinhard Miegel, director of the Institute for Economy and Society in Bonn. "To truly unify two societies . . . requires more than a technocratic financial approach."

Before last year's rush toward reunification, Kohl's political future was in doubt. He had been chancellor since 1982, and Germans seemed weary of his plodding and parochial leadership style. The reunification drama transformed Kohl into a political superstar. He eagerly channeled the euphoria into his own re-election campaign, brushing aside warnings of the potential downside. Now the expectations he raised have been dashed.

[3]Article by Charles Lane from *Newsweek* 117:28–9, Ap 1 '91. Copyright © 1991 Newsweek, Inc. All rights reserved. Reprinted by permission.

Unemployment there is 30 percent and rising; instead of a land of business expansion, the east is actually a slight drag on growth in the west. The cost of unity to the government is now estimated at $600 billion by the year 2000. The fiscally careful Germans, once exporters of capital, are now borrowers.

Kohl's fateful decision was his move last July to convert 160 billion near-worthless East German marks into Deutsche marks at a one-to-one exchange rate. Kohl liked the idea because it would put dramatic new purchasing power in the hands of East German consumers who were about to become all-German voters. But the measure was a disaster for East German industry. Formerly socialist firms lost any price advantage they might have enjoyed over western competitors producing superior goods. And with wages rising, even the most efficient eastern businesses were consigned to instant obsolescence. Western investment has not materialized. Speaking in Brussels last week, Karl Otto Pöhl, the president of Germany's central bank, called the quick monetary union—which he opposed at the time—"a disaster." Kohl bristles at I-told-you-sos: "Nobody could expect us to complete a miracle in six months," he told reporters recently. At a cabinet meeting, the chancellor lashed out at "bad mouthers who always know everything better and never really wanted German unity."

Collective anxiety: Recriminations give little comfort. People in the east have ridden an 18-month roller coaster from the depths of Stalinism to the peak of liberation and down again to economic depression. They are now experiencing a collective case of what the Germans rather vaguely call *Existenzangst*—existential anxiety. Strikes, crime and suicides are spreading, and some of the tension has spilled over into violence: in Dresden last week, right-wing soccer fans attacked players and fans from a visiting Yugoslav team. The erstwhile Communist Free German Youth organization has disintegrated into rival gangs of ultraleftists and cryptofascists. Easterners feel snubbed by "Wessies," who scorn the "shiftlessness" of their poorer cousins and rarely visit the region except to hurtle down the east's autobahns on their way to Berlin. "Why don't they share?" asks an eastern German woman on the train to Leipzig. "The Wessies got everything after the war, and we nothing. We suffered. We're entitled to help."

Kohl and his advisers have begun to acknowledge their mistakes and revise their promises. "We have to admit that we miscalculated and deluded ourselves," said Federal Economics Minister Jürgen Möllemann last week. "There was no way to predict how

much longer it would take to activate self-confidence and entrepreneurial behavior in people who have been deprived of freedom for 58 years." The tax hikes will help meet some of the
increased costs, although another recently floated German idea
for raising money to help the east—trimming Bonn's contribution to the U.S. effort in the gulf—might estrange Kohl further
from his allies.

But Kohl insists that quick reunification was the right course.
Citing the increasingly conservative drift of Soviet policy, he argued last week the policy "was a one-time historical chance, the
opportunity of the moment, whatever you want to call it." Even
Kohl's critics concede that point. For all the woes Germany is
experiencing now, few maintain it would have been better to leave
the Communists in power in the east. Over time the benefits of
reunification, to both east and west, should far outweigh the costs.
Helmut Kohl is betting Germans' patience will ultimately outweigh their *Existenzangst*.

THE HOLLOW SOCIETY[4]

Hermann Looch guides a Western visitor through the new
sewage plant in Ludwiglust, a once sparkling East German town.
"It's the most modern in the country," he says. "Too bad it doesn't
work." The reason: no spare parts. Looch watches with resignation as untreated waste pours into stinking outdoor pools.
"There's nothing to be done. If we're lucky, some West German
company will take us over."

After more than 40 years of communism, East Germany is
imploding. Factories fall apart. Pollution is the worst in Europe.
Thousands flee the country each day—nearly 100,000 so far this
year. And West Germans have come to sift through the ruins.
Fleets of BMWs blow past boxy Trabants on East Germany's autobahns. Rich Düsseldorfers approach East Germans on the street
and ask whether this or that abandoned house might soon be for
sale. For two days in Dresden, a pack of industrialists represent-

[4]Article by Michael Mayer from *Newsweek* 115:26+ F 26 '90. Copyright © 1991
Newsweek, Inc. All rights reserved. Reprinted by permission.

ing 107 companies in West Germany's industrial heartland of Baden-Württemberg garrison the city, pitching deals and buttonholing potential partners. They are offering everything the country needs to rebuild: construction materials, telecommunications equipment, medical supplies. At the bar in the Hotel Bellevue, a West German in a double-breasted Italian suit sits face to face with an East German manager sporting an oddly patterned jacket and white socks. The dialogue is pure Hollywood. "So, you think this 'new thinking' is real?" the West German asks. "For sure," says his counterpart, the manager of a state-owned engineering company. "OK," the West German replies. "My people will call your people."

With the border open, East Germany's vulnerability to business predators is depressingly clear. Eisenhüttenstadt, a.k.a. Iron Works City, was built in the 1950s as a model workers' town, a place where people could create a better life. Modern high-rises were constructed, surrounded by greenery. There were skating rinks, swimming pools and day-care centers for the children; most mothers worked. Today, as elsewhere in East Germany, Eisenhüttenstadt's socialist dream has faded. Houses are shabby and falling into disrepair. Shops are empty save for necessities. People worry about losing their jobs as the town's huge steel industries lose their state subsidies or fall victim to foreign competition. "If the mills go bankrupt," says the editor of the local newspaper, "the city will die."

Death and decay are everyday metaphors. A walk through Weimar, home to Goethe and Schiller, suggests what the country once was. The medieval houses lining its central squares are beautifully restored. But side streets are in ruins. Heaps of coal and garbage lie on shattered pavements. Old-world façades are eroded down to the brick. Every other house seems abandoned. "Don't think they're making repairs," says Heidi Hartmann, watching late-afternoon shoppers take refuge under a scaffold propped up against her crumbling building. "They put it up only after falling stones killed a woman on the street."

'At a loss': The rot goes deeper than decaying walls and empty shops. There is also damage to the soul. After decades of Stalinism, East Germans are hardly ready to become freethinkers. They face the future with trepidation. At Eisenhüttenstadt's technical college, neither professors nor students know quite how to cope. Classes in Marxism-Leninism are out. But what to teach instead? "The faculty is at a loss," says a journalism student.

"After October the dean simply told us to go home. 'Come back when we've figured things out,' he said."

Nor are most East Germans ready to become entrepreneurs. Last month the employees of Erfurt's communist daily, Das Volk, bought out the newspaper and resurrected it as the independent Thüringer Allgemeine. But its future was uncertain. Many staffers worried the newspaper would fail without party support, costing them their jobs. Others objected that new managers might crack down on the party's liberal interpretation of sick leave, reducing workers' time off. In Leipzig, the publisher of a former underground literary journal finds her new freedom positively depressing. In the bad old days, she published 100 *samizdat* copies and distributed them to friends by hand. She figures she could now sell thousands. But finding a printer and "going public," as she calls it, would require too much effort. "I like things better as they are," she says.

Small wonder that so many are leaving. "We have lost more than 200 people," says a railroad conductor—engineers, brakemen, technicians. "Everything is falling apart. The tracks are kaput. The locomotives are breaking down. No one knows what they are supposed to be doing anymore." The receptionist at the town's best hotel says that placing a call across the border takes five hours. An administrator at Weimar's Sophien Hospital reports that a quarter of the staff has left for the West. Doctors and nurses are working double overtime, even subbing as cooks and janitors. "Everyone's exhausted," she says. "It's hard to see how much longer this can go on."

Nowhere is the blight more evident than in Bitterfeld, heart of East Germany's chemical industry. Driving from the West, verdant farmland abruptly drops off into a yawning crevasse—a great coal mine, several miles long and half a mile deep. Excavators like ocean liners tear at the earth. Debris from the pit has been spread across the countryside in huge wind-swept dunes, a sort of man-made Sahara that stretches to the horizon. Bitterfeld lies in the distance, ringed by smokestacks, the sky a dense brown smudge. Locals call their home "the dirtiest city in Europe," but that hardly does justice to this poisoned sinkhole. The incidence of cancer is up. Respiratory diseases are common. Locals go picnicking on the shores of "Silver Lake," so named for the iridescent chemicals dumped there; kids come home from the playground looking like chimney sweeps. Outside the Bitterfeld Red Cross, a West German flag flies. Harald Friedrich, a medical administrator, sums up life in the city. "Lousy," he says. "Maybe things will get better after reunification."

Note that "maybe." East Germany's Communists can be likened to the Roman conquerors of ancient Carthage, who first destroyed the city, then salted the land. Environmentalists agree that Bitterfeld's factories are so hopelessly obsolete that no cleanup is possible unless they are torn down and rebuilt. The same could be said for the rest of the country. A third of the nation's rivers are dead. Air pollution in major cities is 10 to 100 times the safe maximum. Many of the country's houses, bridges and roads have not been repaired since the Communists took power. Where to begin rebuilding when the blight is everywhere? If a unified Deutschland has long been a West German dream, for East Germany it may be the awakening from a nightmare.

DOING BUSINESS IN ONE GERMANY[5]

The two Germanies have been marching toward each other so swiftly and confidently that unification has looked like a parade ground exercise. But when the band strikes up economic unity on July 1, the cadences will get a lot harder to hold. Merging a crumbling Communist economy into a capitalist powerhouse will be like trying to build a Mercedes using parts from the boxy little East German car inelegantly named the Wartburg.

In the long term, the economic payoff ought to be enormous. Western capital and expertise combined with East Germany's skilled, inexpensive work force should result in a thriving West German-style industrial base and a consumer market stretching from the Elbe to the Baltic.

West German companies obviously have the advantage of short supply lines. But there's plenty of opportunity for Americans too. Managers who want to take advantage of what this market offers—hungry consumers, avid workers, access to the Soviet Union—should think through their objectives, fashion a clear strategy, and move fast. Says Hans Fluri, chief financial officer of

[5]Article by Shawn Tully, staffwriter, from *Fortune* 122:80–3. Jl 2 '90. Copyright

Philip Morris's West German subsidiary: "It isn't every day a new market opens up that adds $700 million to our annual sales."

But first comes the hard part. Reviving the flattened East German economy will be expensive—and painful. For many East German workers, the new era will begin with bitter news. East German companies have chosen June 29—the last workday before economic union—to hand out "blue slips," or layoff notices. By some West German estimates, as many as 600,000 workers could be let go.

The big question is how long the grueling transition will take, and you can choose among widely differing opinions. David Kern, chief economist for National Westminster Bank in London, believes that a united Germany faces a decade or more of high budget deficits, inflation, and taxes. "Unification will turn out to be worthwhile in the long run," says Kern, "but it will take up to ten years and maybe longer before we see the gains."

The optimists argue that heavy investment from the West and direct aid from Bonn will get the East German economy rolling as early as next year. Norbert Walter, chief economist for West Germany's Deutsche Bank, predicts that East Germany's gross domestic product will grow at a rapid 7% to 8% annual rate from 1991 to 1995. In recent years, GDP has actually declined.

West German Chancellor Helmut Kohl, the unlikely architect of unification, is siding with the optimists. A plodding conservative, he has surprised even his supporters with his decisiveness and vision. To win over France and other wary neighbors, he has emerged as a champion of European unity—not only the drive for a single market, but the quest for a strong European central government and a single currency as well. Says Henning Christophersen, a European Community official: "German unification is actually speeding up the 1992 process. Kohl has made it clear that a stronger Germany must be anchored in a stronger Europe."

The Kohl government also likes to soft-pedal the power of a united Germany, and it has a point. The new Germany certainly will be bigger, richer, and stronger than today's West Germany. But its might shouldn't be exaggerated. East Germany turns out a gross national product 12% smaller than that of the Netherlands. Even if GNP per capita in the eastern sector eventually reaches West Germany's levels, the economy of the united Germany would still be only 30% as large as that of the U.S.

Kohl has pushed for quick economic union. In May he met

with East German Prime Minister Lothar de Maiziere, a fellow Christian Democrat who had just won the country's first free election, to arrange a treaty merging the two economies by July 1. Kohl's next goal is political union. He wants to unite the two states by this fall, transforming the December elections for the West German Bundestag—the legislative body that chooses the Chancellor—into the first pan-German vote.

By including the East Germans, Kohl would markedly improve his own chances of staying in power. His probable opponent, Social Democrat Oskar Lafontaine, has alienated East German voters by resisting economic union. By contrast, Kohl appears to be popular in the East.

Under the economic treaty, East Germany will adopt the West's free-market system almost intact. Industrial subsidies will stop immediately, and those for housing, mass transit, and heating fuel will be phased out over the next several years. East Germany's feeble currency will be replaced by the deutsche mark on generous terms. Last year it took eight East marks to buy one deutsche mark. On July 1, West Germany will convert most savings—and all wages and pensions—at a rate of one to one.

West Germany's largess only starts with the currency conversion. East Germany faces a severe budget squeeze. In the past it raised 75% of revenues—$123 billion last year—with heavy taxes on state-owned companies, including levies on assets and total wages, as well as producer-paid taxes on consumer goods. In 1991 those taxes will be replaced by a conventional tax on corporate profits, though the rate has not been set. Since most East German companies are losing money, the receipts will be practically nil. In 1991, East Germany's revenues will shrink to an estimated $40 billion.

West Germany has agreed to help cover the budget deficits through 1994. It will borrow most of the money through an international bond issue grandly titled the German Unity Fund. In addition Bonn has to cover its own budget deficit, which will amount to $23 billion in 1991. All told, the two Germanies need to raise $55 billion in 1991, more than three times West Germany's borrowings last year.

Kohl hopes to pay for unification through faster economic growth, not higher taxes. He's counting on the dynamism of the West German economy, aided by a push from the East. According to Deutsche Bank, the combined Germanies should grow at a

strong 3.5% to 4% per year rate from 1991 through 1995. West
Germany grew 3.9% last year. The expansion is supposed to generate a tax revenue windfall in both regions.

Making the strategy work will require a delicate balancing act
by the Bundesbank, now the central bank for both Germanies.
The biggest danger is that old German bugaboo, inflation. The
West German economy is already on the verge of overheating.
Factories are running at full tilt. This year, carmakers and other
employers signed an agreement with the metalworkers' union
that raises wages 6% and shortens the workweek from 37 hours to
35 by 1995.

The huge increase in government spending—and the currency conversion—heightens the risks. Prices could soar if the East
Germans, flush with $71 billion in newly acquired deutsche
marks, splurge on cars and cosmetics. The Kohl government is
hoping that many East Germans will hoard their savings for the
hard times ahead, which seems like a bet against human nature.

Some rise in prices is inevitable. According to Warren Oliver,
an economist with the London investment firm of UBS Phillips &
Drew, inflation will increase from 2.3% today to 3.5% by
mid-1991. "The Bundesbank won't tolerate inflation in the 4%
range," says Oliver. The ever vigilant Bundesbank will tighten the
money supply, lifting interest rates above today's 6% rate and
strengthening the deutsche mark.

The key to the Bundesbank's strategy is a strong deutsche
mark that will make imports less expensive. The central bank is
counting on a large increase in cheaper imports to dampen inflation. That's something new for West Germany, a potent exporter
of both goods and capital. For the next several years, united Germany's imports of products and capital will grow faster than exports. The import explosion should be a boon for the rest of the
world. The European Community projects that unification will
raise its growth rate by half a percentage point a year from 1991
to 1995. The EC should grow 3% this year.

The plan faces two dangers. The cost of unification could be
far higher than Bonn is forecasting. For example, an increase in
unemployment to two million—which is not inconceivable—
could add $6.5 billion to projected annual deficits. And if eco-
nomic revival starts later in East Germany and turns out to
be more sluggish than expected, deficits would grow even
more.

The key is how fast the East German economy can get back on its feet. And that depends on the level of investment. The optimists expect it to be immense. Norbert Walter at Deutsche Bank thinks foreign investment in East Germany could average $30 billion a year for the next decade. To judge just how optimistic that forecast is, consider that Spain, the hottest investment magnet in Europe right now, got just $12 billion last year.

There is, of course, a lot to invest in: East German industry is now up for sale. The best strategy for most Western companies heading East is to buy a stake in an existing East German enterprise or to form a joint venture. Under the Communist regime, the economy was dominated by 170 *Kombinate,* sprawling, state-owned conglomerates that controlled most of the country's manufacturing and service industries. East Germany's newly elected Christian Democratic government is now splitting up the *Kombinate*—as well as smaller regional enterprises—into more than 8,000 Western-style companies owned for now by a new agency called the *Treuhandanstalt,* or Trust. The Trust has a clear mission: privatize East German industry as quickly as possible.

The new companies—many with only a single factory—run the gamut from total deadbeats to a few beauties. Some 2,000 will be shut down, including antiquated, highly polluting plants near Leipzig that make chemicals from soft coal. A handful of star performers, chiefly big exporters to the West, have the choice of becoming independent private companies or picking a foreign partner. A notable example is Planeta, a Dresden-based printing equipment manufacturer that sells $400 million a year of equipment in the U.S., France, and other Western countries.

The vast majority of the remaining companies can't survive on their own. But they have various things that appeal to Western partners. Some can offer good position in potentially lucrative consumer markets. Others have access to the Soviet Union. Many have usable excess production capacity, and most have skilled workers.

Western service companies see a vast serviceless land waiting to be waited on. Hotels are particularly sparse. France's Accor, owner of the Novotel and Sofitel chains, has formed a joint venture with Reiseburo, an East German tour operator, and Interhotels, which operates hotels in major cities. The venture will build hotels from Leipzig to Rostock.

McDonald's plans to blitz the fast-foodless countryside with 100 restaurants, which should generate $100 million in annual sales by the year 2000. And since there is no similar business to join forces with, McDonald's will go it alone.

West German companies are seizing a rare opportunity in machine tools. Capital equipment has long been a big industry for both Germanies, but the two markets have been radically different. West Germany benefits from a big home market and robust exports to the West. Until recently East Germany sent about two-thirds of its machinery to the Soviet Union in exchange for oil. It also exported equipment to the West, generating hard currency to keep its own factories relatively up to date.

But other manufacturers, such as carmakers and chemical producers, could get their hands on little of East Germany's output. And they rarely had enough hard currency to buy equipment abroad. At the Trabant car plant in Zwickau, workers bang shut ill-fitting doors with hammers.

Pent-up demand should lead to an explosive market for machinery. But why not just export to East Germany rather than making a big investment there? One reason is the Soviet connection. Klöckner-Moeller, a West German manufacturer of electric switches and control equipment for machine tools, is taking an equity stake in two factories that produce the same products in East Germany—and do $350 million in sales with the Soviet Union.

There is room for entrepreneurs too. Rainer Pilz, 48, who was born in East Germany, fled to the West and built a consumer electronics business in Munich. Now he has formed a joint venture with Robotron, an East German maker of TVs and other consumer electronics products, to set up a $140 million compact disc factory in Albrechts.

General Motors is heading East for two strategic reasons: The market is huge, and it needs the added production capacity it can get through a joint venture and by building a green-field plant on land that is far cheaper to acquire than in West Germany. By the turn of the century, the market could more than triple to 700,000 cars a year, according to projections by Volkswagen.

At the moment, the East Germans turn out two obsolete models, the Wartburg and the minuscule, smoky Trabant. Later this year GM will start assembling its subcompact Opel Vectra at the Wartburg plant in Eisenach, and it may extend the joint venture by building a new plant to turn out 150,000 cars a year by 1993. Volkswagen has joined Trabant's producer to build a $3 billion assembly plant that will produce 250,000 subcompact Volkswagen Polos a year by 1995.

GM needs to boost capacity because all its European plants are running at full speed. "We're sold out," says Louis Hughes, president of Adam Opel, the company's German subsidiary. In addition to cheaper land, lower wages are an advantage too. Hughes thinks that though East German pay will certainly rise, it could remain below that of West Germany for the short and medium term.

While East Germans haven't been eating Big Macs, they have been smoking and drinking cola for years. So is that a problem for companies like Philip Morris and Coca-Cola? Not much. U.S. consumer giants have a tremendous advantage in fame and quality. Since the market opened in April, sales of Marlboro and other Philip Morris brands have jumped from $2 million a month to $35 million. Smokers didn't need big ad campaigns to switch from local brands made from smelly Bulgarian tobacco.

Philip Morris has agreed to purchase East Germany's largest cigarette plant, based in Dresden. Besides producing its own brands, the company will strive to improve the existing ones—no doubt looking beyond Bulgaria for raw materials. Philip Morris is taking over on generous terms. It has agreed to raise salaries 12%, to an average of $8,900 a year, and keep all of the 1,000 workers at least until 1992.

Coke was, in a sense, presold. Says Heinz Wiezorek, president of the company's West German subsidiary: "East Germans have been hearing about Coke for years on West German TV." Wagner's Beverage Corner, a store in East Berlin, now sells 30 cases of Coke a week, vs. 24 cases of the local-brand Club Cola—even though heavily subsidized Club sells at a quarter of Coke's price. Measured in cases, sales of Coca-Cola are already one-sixth the level in West Germany.

That could put some extra sparkle in Coca-Cola's earnings: The West German market accounts for 12% of the company's profits, or $200 million last year. Over the next few years Coca-Cola will invest $140 million in East Germany to upgrade its bottling and distribution systems.

The two Germanies are joining hands in an unprecedented economic experiment. Months or even years of pain lie ahead. The free market will do its work with savage efficiency. When the storm settles on German economic union, the territory that was once East Germany will be reborn as a beacon to the Communist world and a strong partner to the West.

LETTER FROM GERMANY[6]

I'm just back from Dresden and some factory towns in East Germany—Saxony today—and Wolfsburg (the Volkswagen works), Ingolstadt (the Audi factories) and Munich in the West. You've been reading how difficult it's going to be for the East Germans to adjust after 45 years of "you pretend to pay us, we pretend to work" communism, how much unemployment there is and will be, how the West Germans were tired of paying the bills for the East. I'm just back from a visit to Germany, East and West, and I have a contrary tale to tell.

Zwickau in the East. We toured the old Trabant plant. There are 9,300 workers building 200 Trabants a day on two shifts. In the United States, by contrast, from 1,500 to 2,300 workers will assemble 50 to 60 cars an hour. The Trabant technology is decades old, and the 200-a-day production is part of a 35,000-car order from Poland and Hungary. No one else would buy the junk.

On the surface, the factory and the car are laughable. Reporters from the *New York Times* and the *Wall Street Journal* laughed at this symbol of terrible productivity. But I've seen a lot of car plants, probably more than the rest of the group put together. Let me tell you about this one:

It was old but clean. The machinery was ancient, but it was working. Someone was keeping that stuff running. There was a huge work force, 9,300, but they had to do just about everything. When a forklift broke, they had to make the parts themselves in order to fix it. They weren't working very hard, but they kept things running.

To me these are the signs of a lousy system but a competent, mechanically adept work force.

We went a few miles down the road to visit an engine plant. That plant, with those same East German workers, is now making vw engines that are sent back West. That means they are up to

[6]Article by Jerry Flint, staff writer, from *Forbes* 146:72–3, 76 O 29, '90. Reprinted by permission of FORBES magazine © Forbes Inc., 1990.

West German quality. Production is building up. Six months ago 28 parts of that vw engine were imported from West Germany. Today only 3 parts are imported. The vw Golf models built in the West German plant at Wolfsburg have headlights made in East Germany; the new presses in the Wolfsburg plant are from the East. All this means that the East German supplier base is building. Faster than most people expected.

We went to the new vw assembly plant complex going up in nearby Mosel. East German work crews are putting together a few vw Polos a day, learning modern assembly methods. The foremen are explaining things; the work crews look spiffy and soak it up. It's slow going, but there's still a world of difference from the Trabant plant. They are digging holes for the allied stamping and parts plants that will be part of this complex. In three years, vw says, it will build 250,000 cars a year with 7,000 workers. The old Trabant plant will probably build axles and other parts.

The East Germans earn less than a third the pay of a Volkswagen worker in the West, and probably aren't worth that on the basis of today's productivity (although they have a 42-hour workweek, compared with 37.5 in the West). But now the East Germans are getting paid in real money. Believe me, teaching these guys how to work in a modern environment will be a piece of cake. They all can read and write. You want to hear about problems, ask Lee Iacocca about what it's like to run an inner-city plant where half the workers are illiterate. That's a problem. This, in East Germany, is an opportunity.

We traveled the roads of East Germany. They were filled with big cars, Mercedes, bmws. I thought the cars all belonged to tourists from West Germany, visiting relatives. Wrong. The East Germans bought the cars, used, from West Germans. Shouldn't they want small cars? "No, they like a V-8. Small cars they have driven all their lives," laughed Ulrich Seiffert, the head of research and development at Volkswagen.

Unemployment? They will need thousands of workers, thousands, just to man the new gasoline stations and garages they need to build in East Germany to keep all those extra cars (half a million cars moved East the past few months) filled up and running.

Another thing: We've been saying how poor the East Germans would be when food prices and rent went up. But consumer durables are unbelievable bargains for the East Germans.

"Not a TV set for 9,000 marks, now it's 800 marks; not 120,000 marks for a terrible car, 8,000 for a used VW," says Carl Hahn, the chairman of Volkswagen. "They waited 15 years for a car that was below human dignity almost. They waited 6 years to get a vacant [vacation] bed on the Baltic. Now, 2,300 marks from here to Hawaii. Incredible."

Carl Hahn was born in Saxony near those East German car plants I visited. He says the trade schools of the East are still operating and turning out skilled workers, even if in the past the schools had ancient equipment and socialism to bog them down. But they are skilled workers. Volkswagen's Hahn is betting DM 5 billion ($3 billion) on it, for those new plants I saw under construction and the training. Carl Hahn is no fool. He's the man who came to the United States three decades ago and put Volkswagen on the map with the famous "Think Small" advertising campaigns and the emphasis on quality service. Now he sees an enormous boom tied to those 16 million East Germans coming home.

We walked around Dresden. Still a bit of damage to be repaired, still some wrecked buildings, empty lots. But that's not a minus, that's a plus. They need repairs to the public buildings. They need telephones. They need roads and apartments. There's plenty of investment capital. This spells boom to me.

I lived in Germany for two years while I was in the U.S. Army in 1954–56. Much of the place was still rubble. But the Germans were working, oh, how they worked. I will never forget my first German morning, in Mannheim, looking out the window and seeing a skyline filled with cranes. For two years I watched them struggling. Rebuilding. Men, women. That's the way Germans are. They work. Even 45 years under a communist government doesn't change that. They are still Germans, with the traits we hate and the traits we admire. They work.

I would predict that in 18 months the skylines of Dresden, Leipzig, Berlin, etc., will be a line of cranes and that there will be the beginnings of a labor shortage, and that in three years there will be a labor shortage.

Munich was another shock, but of a different sort. Never, nowhere, have I seen such concentrated wealth in about two square miles as I saw in Munich. Part of this was the stores, the stores filled with the booty of the earth, on the streets and in cleverly designed mazes. Part of it was the people, so rich and fat (in the Biblical sense). Part of it was that it all seemed to work. The city looked like a city. It was clean. Traffic moved, the public transit looked good. I tell you, Detroit and Munich, even New York and Munich, aren't on the same planet. What have we been doing all these years, I thought.

You hear about the costs of reunification, $8 billion to buy the Russians out, billions more for something else. It's peanuts. Say there are 9 million people working again in the East German states, say the average production potential might be $30,000 per person (just a guess, but it is a very low guess). That multiplies out to a production potential of close to $300 billion a year! That makes the price paid for reunification very minor.

Well, yes, the Germans have problems. The big worry of the Europeans is that the Japanese are coming, little cars against vw and Opel, big Toyota Lexus models to knock the stuffing out of Mercedes and BMW and Audi. The Germans will take some knocks from the Japanese, I think, but they'll keep the Japanese down with quotas for 5 or 10 years. We're not sowing a new Europe just to let the Japanese reap the first harvest, Hahn said. A big problem is the high German labor costs, about $65,000 a year per man in wages and social benefit costs. They've got a 7½-hour day. They actually work 8 hours, but get 17 extra days off to make up for the extra half-hour. Hahn says they tell the unions of the problems, but then the unions just point at those big trade balances and the climbing dividends. "Somehow we manage," he says.

And they do. And they will manage East Germany. I've seen them rebuild. You bet against the Germans if you want to. I won't.

II. IMMIGRATION AND MINORITIES

EDITOR'S INTRODUCTION

Section Two of this compilation focuses on immigration into West Germany, partly from East Germany but also from ethnic Germans living formerly in eastern Europe and in the Soviet Union. In one respect, the influx of these people has been fortunate, providing an enlarged labor force when it is needed. In another respect, however, the surge of immigration has become nearly too large to handle, straining West Germany's housing and social services to the breaking point. The large-scale immigration has also angered West German unions, which fear that their contract demands will be jeopardized; and in some sectors, the foreigners, who may prove difficult to assimilate, have incited resentment.

In the first article in this section, Russell Watson writing in *Newsweek* comments on the crisis in East Germany just after the opening of the Berlin Wall. Despite constant surveillance by the state security police, defections to West Germany had assumed epidemic proportions, draining the East of its young people, its skilled as well as unskilled workers, and inundating West Germany with immigrants numbering in the hundreds of thousands. A following article by Robert Kaplan in the *Atlantic* notes that most of the immigrants to West Germany are not from East Germany but rather from the Soviet Union, Yugoslavia, Hungary, and Czechoslovakia. In a related article, George Epp in the *Christian Century* discusses the ethnic German migration more fully, noting that the influx of these settlers, previously welcomed by the West German officials, has reached such proportions that public sentiment is increasing to restrict immigration. Finally, also in *Christian Century,* John Schmidt discusses the situation of Jews living in East and West Germany. In West Germany the community of 6,000 Jews has been widely respected and consulted, but the much smaller community in East Germany has been experiencing some anxiety with an upsurge of anti-Semitic activity.

A SOCIETY DEEP IN CRISIS[1]

Ingo Kargel, a 17-year-old East Berliner, made the long jour-
ney to freedom last month—through Czechoslovakia to Hungary
and then on to West Germany. Eventually he arrived at a refugee
center on the edge of West Berlin, having traveled 1,500 miles to
end up a few hundred yards from where he began. Last Thursday night [mid-November 1989], Kargel learned that thousands
of East Germans were coming straight through the wall, leaving
the German Democratic Republic (GDR) in the easiest way possible. "I'm very shocked and a little bit sad," he said as he thought
it over. "Did I leave my homeland too early? If the GDR opened
the gates, it's not the GDR I knew."

It's no longer the GDR anyone knew. "East Germany is
awakening," the Communist Party's Central Committee said as it
tried to scramble onto the bandwagon. "A revolutionary people's
movement has set in motion a process of serious upheaval." Suddenly their rulers were promising East Germans almost anything.
The Central Committee's "action program" specified "free, general, democratic and secret elections." It called for "radical disarmament" and "freedom of information and the media." It promised to overhaul the rust-bucket economy, with a special emphasis
on producing consumer goods. All this and travel, too. Egon
Krenz, the new leader whose doctrinaire rigidity has suddenly
given way to pliability, said the party had learned "a major
lesson": that, given the freedom to travel, most East Germans
would visit the West and willingly return home.

Has a brutal police state been transformed into an open society? Among the thousands of East Germans who poured across
the border after the restrictions on travel were lifted, a small
minority planned to stay in the West. "We have absolutely no
confidence in Krenz," Walter Kolbow, a young father from Mag-
deburg, said as he changed his daughter's diapers at a refugee
center near the Czech border. "It will be 20 years before life in the

[1]Article by Russell Watson, staffwriter, from *Newsweek* 114:31–2 N 20 '89.

GDR resembles that in the Federal Republic," said another refugee, a 25-year-old man from the Baltic region. "I do not want to wait." East Germany is an Orwellian society in a profound state of crisis. "This damned bureaucratic regulation . . . has ruined us," Hans Modrow, the new, reform-minded Communist prime minister said recently. Even before the barriers came tumbling down, 225,000 East Germans had left their country for good so far this year. "We figure there is a 500,000 ceiling," says a Western diplomat in East Berlin. "After that, this place will collapse."

East Germany may already have changed beyond the capacity of any hardliner to reimpose absolute tyranny. In one remarkable week, Krenz's regime sacked the cabinet, shuffled the Politburo and aligned itself, belatedly, with the reform campaign of Soviet leader Mikhail Gorbachev. Across Eastern Europe, the pace of change seems to have accelerated beyond almost anyone's control. In Poland last week, Solidarity leader Lech Walesa left for Canada and the United States to drum up aid for his country's emerging democracy. There were stirrings in the deepest backwaters of communist orthodoxy. Bulgarian President Todor Zhivkov, the senior leader in the Soviet bloc, abruptly resigned after 35 years in power. His 53-year-old successor, Petar Mladenov—like Krenz a long-time apparatchik—said there was "no alternative" to reform, though "only within the framework of socialism."

Unlike their counterparts in Poland or Hungary, many reform-minded East Germans are not anti-communist, at least not yet. Their campaign for change is not so much a revolution as a civil-rights movement. Most East German reformers want to improve socialism and exercise the rights they are entitled to in theory. The failures of socialism are blamed on Erich Honecker, Krenz's fallen mentor, and on other leaders of the government apparatus and the ruling Socialist Unity Party (SED), as the Communists are known.

"The leading role of the Socialist Unity Party doesn't exist anymore," says Manfred Gerlach, leader of the Liberal Democratic Party, which until recently was a junior partner of the Communists and now is trying to spread its own wings. Gerlach argues that "despite the problems, socialism has also brought many achievements to this country. We have social security, no unemployment, low inflation—this is the result of socialist development." He notes that, "In the entire world, there are no better-fed or better-dressed refugees" than the East Germans who have gone West. "They arrive in their own cars," he says. "And once the stagnation and encrustation have been dealt with, I don't know why people would reject socialism here."

By opening the gates to emigration, the regime has ensured that many of its most extreme opponents will leave and that most of those who remain will be devoted to socialism, if not to Soviet-style communism. Rank-and-file reformers can use a kind of civic blackmail to promote change. At a huge demonstration in Leipzig recently, the crowd chanted: "In one day, I can be out of here." Those who choose not to leave generally are committed to socialist ideals. Last week a group of writers and opposition figures signed an appeal urging people to stay in the country. "What can we promise you? Nothing easy, to be sure, but an interesting and useful life," said novelist Christa Wolf, who read the document on TV. "No quick riches, but a chance to participate in great changes," she said.

That sort of argument appeals even to some anti-communists. "People who leave make things too easy for themselves," said an electrical engineer who demonstrated in Leipzig. "It makes more sense for me to stay here and work for change. We need to have free elections and let the people decide if they want the SED to lead them. I know [the Communists] wouldn't win."

It is still difficult for many East Germans to trust their leaders or to believe that things have changed for good. The Communists have ruled through intimidation and mind control. Their prime instruments are the hated Stasi, the plainclothes state-security police whose official task is to "protect socialism." Stasi spies are rumored to infest nearly every office, factory, apartment building and schoolhouse. The authorities have turned the educational system, once a source of socialist enlightenment, into a tool of repression, a world of rote learning and unbending doctrine, where creativity and spontaneity are politically suspect.

Amid last week's euphoria, many East Germans finally began to shake off the feeling that someone was watching—and recording their transgressions. Only a few weeks ago, during a demonstration in Dresden, one small group of protesters talking to a foreign journalist kept nudging one another and casting sidelong glances at a couple standing nearby, who looked equally uneasy. It turned out that both groups were ordinary demonstrators; each thought the other was spying on them. When the misunderstanding became clear, nervous laughter broke out on both sides. A man from one group approached a man from the other and patted him on the back. The two embraced in a quick, embarrassed hug of relief.

At the big demonstration in Leipzig, people derided the police, chanting: "Stasi, go to work," and "Shame on you." Some of them were indeed put to work, driving buses and trucks left idle by the flood of workers to the West. With thousands of East Germans leaving their country every day, the hard-hit economy needs more help than that. Food and other scarce commodities have been piling up at warehouses because so many truck drivers have disappeared. Industrial managers complain that they cannot get the parts and materials they need to keep operating. Store windows in East Berlin are plastered with "Help Wanted" signs. The manager of a Dresden factory's soccer team complains that when his players went on holiday to Czechoslovakia, only half of them returned to work. "How can you run a factory," he asks, "when you do not know how many of your employees and managers will show up each morning?"

At Schirnding in Bavaria, the main crossing point from Czechoslovakia to West Germany, a quick survey turns up many well-trained refugees: carpenters, engineers, dentists, truck drivers, schoolteachers, bakers, cooks, dishwashers and steelworkers. Doctors and nurses are leaving East Germany in especially large numbers because of their vastly better earning prospects in the West. East German doctors earn less than $1,000 a month, about the same as a bus driver, except that a bus driver gets an extra five days off. Even before travel restrictions were eliminated, doctors were leaving the country at a rate of 60 a month. A third of the physicians at Magdeburg's prestigious medical academy failed to come back from their summer vacations. In Wittenberg, the city's hospital for the disabled may have to close because of staff losses. "We have only one nurse to every 40 patients," says hospital director Ernst Petzhold.

West German authorities predict that between 1 million and 2 million of East Germany's 16.6 million people eventually will leave their country. If so, East Germany will lose up to 20 percent of its work force. "It will be very hard," says a doctor at the Invalidenstrasse crossing in West Berlin. "The economy is weak enough now. Such an exodus would cripple it."

The current exodus already threatens to overwhelm West Germany, which promises citizenship and support to any ethnic German who comes to claim it. Shelters are overflowing with refugees for whom jobs and homes are scarce. The city of Frankfurt virtually closed its doors to new refugees last week. Hamburg considered housing them in steel cargo containers, while Bremen wanted to put them into air-raid shelters. When Bonn announced an emergency $4.3 billion home-building plan, critics said it was too modest. Ralf Schlichting, spokesman for West Berlin's housing authority, said the city's share of the money would be "enough to build only 350 two- or three-room flats. What we need are 30,000 flats right now, and another 100,000 in four years' time." Then he corrected himself; 100,000 was the projection before the East opened its gates. "Perhaps we need half a million now," he said. "Who knows?"

"It's not a problem to give people a bed," said Harald Fiss, director of West Berlin's biggest refugee-reception center. "It's a problem to integrate them. In the cities, the flats are full. Kindergartens are full. All people want to go to the big cities to find jobs. They should go to the countryside." West German Interior Minister Wolfgang Schäuble warned would-be immigrants last week that their living conditions in West Germany might be worse than what they had at home. Some native West Germans resent the intrusion from the East. Their unemployment rate already stands at more than 7 percent of the work force—nearly 2 million people—and they don't want more competition. "West Berlin is full," complains Caroline Braband, a worker at the city's Adoros Halle refugee center. "A lot of people come here and think they are the boss," she claims. "They want to get and get and get. They don't think they have to work for it."

Some East Germans may want to work in the West without living there, creating a new "guest worker" problem and displacing workers that have been imported from countries like Turkey. A 20-year-old East German bartender had been planning to emigrate via Czechoslovakia last Friday. Then the wall opened up on Thursday. "I was just about finished with this country, but now I don't know," he said as he prepared to cross the border that night. "I just want to go over there and see what it is like. Maybe I can get a job over there and continue to live here. Housing is cheap [in East Germany], and the benefits are good."

If the party's promises can be taken at face value, East Germany soon will become more like the West, at least in terms of its political arrangements. The "action program" published by the Central Committee implied a turn toward socialist democracy, calling for "a democratic coalition government." East Berlin party chief Günter Schabowski even hinted that the Communists might allow themselves to be voted out of power. At a rally outside party headquarters, Krentz told the faithful: "We want a socialism that is economically effective, politically democratic, morally clean and, most of all, has its face turned toward the people." But the party did not explicitly promise to surrender its "leading role" in the country, or to give up power peacefully if voted out of office. "If the party starts treating us like people, instead of children, that will be very nice," a middle-aged East German said near the Brandenburg Gate. "But it is too early to tell what might come."

By allowing free travel, Krenz stayed one step ahead of a political avalanche. After a career in the hard-line party bureaucracy, he suddenly repositioned himself as a reformer. He could yet become East Germany's Gorbachev. "If the GDR follows the path of Hungary and Poland," said one East German, "Krenz will become genuinely popular with the people."

So far, however, there was no assurance that Krenz meant to emulate the Hungarians or the Poles. People remembered his 15-year affiliation with the discredited Honecker. They remembered that for years he was in charge of the security apparatus. They remembered that, only last June, he endorsed China's bloody crackdown against its own democracy movement. "A leopard doesn't change his spots," sneered an East Berliner. "Krenz is only reforming because he has to."

He also faces dissent in his own party. An increasingly independent and reform-minded Central Committee rejected three of Krenz's nominees to the Politburo last week because they were too closely tied to the old-guard regime. Reformers within the SED will press their case at a party conference hurriedly scheduled for next month. Meanwhile, Hans Modrow, the reformist nominee for prime minister, seems much more popular than his boss; it is Modrow's name, not Krenz's, that people chant in the streets. When he was party chief in Dresden, Modrow made a name for himself by listening to what workers had to say and by shunning the perks that went with his office (he drove his own car and lived in a simple apartment instead of the official villa). He was so popular and so committed to change that his career appeared to be going nowhere. As his star suddenly rose to the Politburo last week, Modrow called for free elections and a multiparty democracy. "Our leader must face the people's demands," he said.

Many opposition figures, including members of New Forum, the largest group, are not optimistic about the prospects for thorough reform led by the Communists. Steffen Reiche, a leader of the fledgling Social Democratic Party, which aspires to be the political arm of New Forum, says the system is "nearing collapse. The Communist Party isn't in a position to manage this reform," he says. "They talk about a *Wende,* or turnaround, but what good is turning in a swamp?" Like many critics of the regime, Reiche wants to preserve socialism in a separate East Germany. If Krenz wants to accomplish that—and retain his own grip on power—he will have to follow his opening of the wall with another stunning reform: truly democratic elections.

THE LOST SHEEP[2]

When the children of medieval Hamelin, in Lower Saxony, were led underground by the legendary Pied Piper, they reemerged a thousand miles to the southeast, deep in the Carpathian Mountains, not far from the Black Sea. The fable, immortalized by Johann Wolfgang von Goethe, the brothers Grimm, and Robert Browning, has historical roots in the twelfth-century German colonization of Transylvania, which was then in Hungary and is now in Romania. Summoned by the Magyar King, Géza II, to protect Hungary's eastern flank against the Byzantine Empire, the German immigrants in Transylvania founded what came to be known as the *Siebenbürgen,* or seven cities. To this day these fortified towns—despite the Romanian appellations on international maps—are known to all Germans by the grave Teutonic peal of the names the settlers gave them: for example, Kronstadt (Braşov), Klausenburg (Cluj-Napoca), Hermannstadt (Sibiu), Schässburg (Sighişoara). Such was the impression left on visitors by these dour, hardworking German immigrants that when Jonathan Harker, in Bram Stoker's novel *Dracula,* travels east through Transylvania to Count Dracula's castle, he naturally is said to alight at a town whose name is rendered not as Romanians

[2]Article by Robert D. Kaplan, freelance writer, from *The Atlantic* 265:26–8 N '90. Copyright © 1990 by *The Atlantic.* Reprinted by permission.

or Hungarians would have it but rather as Germans do: "Klausenburg."

Ethnic German youths in Romania served in large numbers in the Waffen-SS as German forces swept across Eastern Europe during the Second World War. One ethnic German from Romania I spoke with last year remembers the early years of the war, when she was a young girl, as a time of "no poverty, of a protected social structure." She says, "We had a nice house and garden in Kronstadt, a very *bürgerlich* [bourgeois] life-style. My father sang in the church choir. We put on our own Wagner operas." The "breaking point" in her life, from good to bad, she told me, came in 1945, after the Nazis withdrew from Transylvania.

Russian soldiers, bayonets drawn, entered her home, taking her father and fifteen-year-old brother away to forced-labor camps. Her brother escaped. Her father died soon thereafter, while working in the mines of the Donets Basin, in the southern Soviet Union. Only in 1973 was the family officially notified of his death. The years between, under the Communist Romanian government, saw an unsparing procession of suffering. The woman and her relatives were evicted from their house and made to share a single room for fourteen years, with no private kitchen or bathroom. There were chronic food shortages. The Germans' culture and dialect were suppressed. In 1979, after much official harassment, the woman, her husband, and their two sons were allowed to emigrate, without any possessions, to West Germany; the government of West Germany for years paid Romania more than $4,000 for each exit visa that it granted to an ethnic German. "Believe me, I know what it is to be German," the woman, nearly in tears, said to me.

Multiply her story by 3.5 million and you will begin to grasp the significance of a variable that could powerfully influence the evolution of West Germany—and of Germany as a whole. For obvious reasons the world's attention has recently been drawn to the exodus of hundreds of thousands of East Germans to West Germany, to the tearing-down of parts of the Berlin Wall, and to the suddenly brighter prospects for some sort of future German unification. The existence of large numbers of ethnic Germans beyond the borders of either of the Germanys is a quieter issue, but among Germans everywhere it possesses great emotional force, and it figures large in West Germany's domestic politics and foreign policy.

The largest number of ethnic Germans outside Germany—some two million of them—live in the Soviet Union; many are descendants of settlers lured to Russia in the eighteenth and nineteenth centuries by Catherine the Great and Czar Alexander I to populate regions conquered from Turks and Crimean Tartars. Hundreds of thousands of these Russian Germans now live in Siberia and Central Asia, to which they were brutally evacuated from European Russia and the Volga region by Stalin's secret police after the Nazi invasion. Today they and their offspring live side by side with ethnic Uzbeks and Tadzhiks in grim, crowded apartment blocks. I interviewed several ethnic German refugees from the city of Dushanbe, in Tadzhikistan, not far from the Afghan border. They spoke good German, albeit with a distinct Russian accent. By speaking only German at home with their children, and regularly attending Catholic Church services with other ethnic Germans, they had been able to preserve their cultural identity.

Outside the Soviet Union there are a million Germans living in western Poland, in what were the Reich provinces of Pomerania and Silesia until Poland was displaced westward after the Second World War. And Germans are scattered throughout Yugoslavia, Hungary, Czechoslovakia, and what used to be East Prussia (now northeast Poland and Soviet Kaliningrad).

These ethnic Germans have a proud, unambiguous sense of national identity, one that has been tempered by the experience of exile and persecution. And many of them are coming home. "The lost sheep are being brought back to the Promised Land," observes Ingeborg Fleischhauer, an expert on German minorities who lives in Bonn. "The ethnic-German exodus from the Soviet Union is running larger than that of the Jews in the 1970s. It is the biggest legal emigration in Soviet history." Last year 377,000 ethnic Germans emigrated to West Germany from the Soviet Union and Eastern European countries other than East Germany—30,000 more than the number who emigrated from East Germany during last year's celebrated influx.

"We should thank God for these people," Fleischhauer says. "It is as if they come from heaven. They are a solution to all our problems." Until recently the Federal Republic's population, now 61 million, was declining; France, with 56 million people, was poised to overtake West Germany by the turn of the century. But the immigrants have stabilized West Germany's population. The newcomers will help solve the manpower problem that the

Federal Republic's armed forces, the Bundeswehr, was expecting to face in coming years. They will fill blue-collar jobs that West Germans don't seem to want. And their desire to work and to consume, after years of communist torpor, will, according to some experts, sustain West Germany's already long postwar economic boom.

"The new settlers will change Germany just as the millions of other immigrants from the East changed Germany after World War Two," predicts Hartmut Koschyk, the general secretary of Der Bund der Vertriebenen (The League of Expellees), the most important of several pro-immigration lobbying organizations in West Germany. In the war's aftermath some fourteen million ethnic Germans fled from their homes before advancing Soviet armies, or were driven from them by angry, vengeful local populations. They were condemned to plod west, through winter snows, across hundreds of miles of devastated Eastern European landscape. Two million Germans perished, mainly women and children. Given that many ethnic Germans collaborated with the Nazis, compassion for the refugee "Volksdeutsche" was lacking in the late 1940s. Their displacement, however, represented the largest movement of population in European history. It was the arrival of at least 12 million of these people in West Germany, many economists believe, that gave the West German economy a crucial jump start.

The economic implications of the newest wave of immigration, however, remain a matter of debate; the influx of East German refugees late last year and the uncertain character of West Germany's relations with its fraternal neighbor, among other things, cloud the picture. In any event, few in West Germany doubt that the social and psychological consequences of the immigration will be as important as the economic ones.

Simon Wiesenthal, a Jewish concentration-camp survivor and the Vienna-based hunter of Nazi war criminals, believes that the new wave of immigration can only fortify West German democracy. He looks back at the way a war-smashed Germany gave succor to 12 million refugees from the East. A refusal or inability to do so, he observes, would have caused enormous and protracted problems (consider, he says, the consequences of the Arab refusal to embrace refugee Palestinians); but Germany extended its hand, and came to a moral turning point. It was an act of generosity, all the more important because the generosity was largely automatic, and was offered by a population that lacked the means to feed and clothe even itself, let alone hordes of newcomers.

More problematic, the new immigrants—including the recent East German arrivals—are living proof to West Germans that "Germany" is a concept that extends far beyond the borders of the Federal Republic, or even of West and East Germany together. The ethnic Germans are bringing West Germans face to face with a troublesome past. They use words that went unspoken in the homeland for decades, because of their association with the Nazis: words like *Volk* (people, nation, or tribe) and *Reich* (empire). Old maps seem to have emerged from nowhere. One sees them not only at the immigrant associations but also in West German government offices and border-police headquarters, and even foreign embassies. Germany on these maps is a fearsome bulge of territory stretching from France to Lithuania. It includes all of West and East Germany, and most of western and northeastern Poland; gray islands throughout Eastern Europe denote ethnic-German settlement areas. Handing me several such maps, Hartmut Koschyk, of the League of Expellees, made sure to emphasize the existence of "German lands inside the present Polish state." Another league official refers to East Germany as "Middle Germany," explaining that the "real Eastern" Germany is in Poland and the Baltic states. Detlef Kühn, the president of the All-German Institute, in Bonn, says, "For decades the Cold War cut us off from the East, but now Germans are resuming their interest." Kühn notes that "there was never a formal peace treaty after the war, and the German Reich as it existed in 1937 still constitutes the just and legal boundaries of Germany." He adds that the Federal Republic's Basic Law of 1949, which established the boundaries of West Germany around the American, British, and French occupation zones, was meant to be only "temporary."

Technically, Koschyk and Kühn are right. But as other Germans have pointed out, arguments like theirs promote a state of affairs that, given the legacy of Nazi rule, is simply unacceptable to the outside world. In an interview shortly before his death, Hoimar von Ditfurth, who was a professor at the University of Heidelberg and an active supporter of West Germany's left-wing Green Party, told me that he saw people like Koschyk and Kühn as representing "a core of reaction that is unable to learn anything from history."

Nevertheless, the immigrant associations are emblematic of a certain drift in West German politics. They occupy the right flank of Chancellor Helmut Kohl's right-of-center Christian Democrat-

ic Union. And as nearly everyone in Bonn will tell you, it is right-
ward that Kohl is headed, in order to steal the thunder of the
Republicans, a new extremist party vaguely reminiscent of a neo-
Nazi movement. The Republicans won 7.1 percent of the German
vote in last year's European parliamentary elections. It is thus no
accident that Kohl's CDU pampers groups like The League of
Expellees, giving them money to publish more books, brochures,
and maps. Wolfgang G. Gibowski, a Mannheim-based political
pollster, says that "national feeling in West Germany is stronger
than you may want to believe."

The Germans from the Soviet Union, Romania, Poland, and
elsewhere will be more important than the East German refugees
in determining the future character of the new nationalism in
Germany. The East Germans are escaping communism; the ethnic Germans are escaping not only communism but also discrimination against them as Germans. They have a much better developed sense of German nationalism than the East Germans do,
and their lobbying mechanism in Bonn has been in operation for
four decades.

The eventual reunification of East and West Germany is already taken for granted by many. The big question remaining is
whether that enlarged future Germany will be neutral or part of
an expanded North Atlantic Treaty Organization. But Germany's
relationship—both political and psychological—with its lost territories to the east will take longer to work out. Even after the
current migration of ethnic Germans slows, between one and two
million of them are expected to remain in Eastern Europe. And
their immigrant relatives in West Germany will make sure that
Bonn—or Berlin—doesn't ever forget them.

A MIXED WELCOME FOR RETURNING GERMANS[3]

A neighbor bends my ear for a good half hour while I edge
closer to the front door of the apartment, my bag of groceries

[3]Article by George Epp, staff writer, from *Christian Century* 106:902–3 O 11, '89.
Copyright 1989 Christian Century Foundation. Reprinted by permission.

getting heavier by the minute. "I don't know why all the Germans want to come to this country," he says. He himself is one of the "Germans" from East Europe who trickled into the Federal Republic during the 1970s. Somehow he has quickly made the switch from immigrant to native when thinking about his own situation.

"Many are saying this fulfills the Old Testament prophecy that says that in the end times people will return to their own nations," he says, "but I think it's maybe an example of Jesus' saying that if, like a son repeatedly begging his father for something, you pray to God for years, he finally gives in, if just to end your persistent begging."

It's a simple precept, but why not? People whose survival has routinely been in doubt probably have more use for simple than for complex explanations, and simple precepts and simple rhetoric underlie the fever of emigration out of East Europe among people claiming Germanic roots. Germany is their home; the U.S.S.R., Poland and Romania are lands of exile; they must go home before the doors close again and trap them and their children in who knows what further horror. The trickle has become a stream, the stream a flood. In 1962 the total emigration of Germanic peoples from East Europe (including East Germany) was about 32,000. In 1970, it was 40,000. In 1988, as a result of *glasnost,* the number very nearly reached 200,000. By current projections, the number in 1989 might well be 400,000. Since 1961, nearly 2 million have come, nearly half from Poland and a similar number from the U.S.S.R., with the remainder from Yugoslavia, Romania, Czechoslovakia and Hungary. It has become one of history's greatest migrations, equivalent to the movement of Irish to North America during the 1850 famine or the exit of the middle class from South Vietnam after the fall of Saigon.

But this is a quiet migration, or at least it was until this past year when the numbers of arrivals in the Federal Republic of Germany severely strained the country's ability to receive them. Reception centers in Friedland, Unna-Massen and Osnabrück are handling twice as many people as they can comfortably process, and the clamor for housing has driven up prices and soured the market for all German apartment hunters. Add to this the usual resentment against immigrants competing with citizens for jobs, and it becomes clear why some native Germans are voicing opposition to their government's generous acceptance of these *Umsiedler,* or resettlers.

The reception is generous. Once a German family in the U.S.S.R. has gained an exit visa from Moscow—producing an invitation from a relative abroad is the key—a plane ticket to Frankfurt and a wait for a seat will fulfill the dream. Upon arrival they must satisfy the immigration authorities that they are either a *Staatsangerhöriger* (one who had and never voluntarily relinquished German citizenship) or a *Volkszugehöriger* (one who has remained a member of a group that retained its German culture and language and defined itself as "German"), or a spouse of one of the above. Then a resettler is paid a flat fee called "welcome money," which could amount to several thousand German marks for a family. They might also receive reparation payments for every working year in East Europe, which could reach tens of thousands of marks, plus full access to pension, health care and social-services benefits. Many resettlers achieve a standard of living equal to or exceeding that of their neighbors in a matter of a few years.

Who is German?" people are beginning to ask. Can those who have lived as Soviet citizens all their lives and have up to ten generations of ancestors who have lived on Russian soil really be considered German? And what about those who took Polish names in self-defense, forgot the German language and culture and are now apparently using the system to emigrate from a difficult economic situation? Do they have a claim to German citizenship?

The West German government of Chancellor Helmut Kohl has put a great deal of effort into convincing voters that the resettlers are kinfolk—that they are not Poles, Soviets or Romanians, but Germans. But it's an uphill battle at a time when the social and political resistance to allowing any more people into the Federal Republic is growing, spurred on most recently by the flood of East Germans coming through a liberalized Hungary. Contributing to the widespread suspicion of immigrants is residual irritation over the thousands of Turkish "guest workers" who never went home. East Germans are obviously German, in the eyes of the general population, but they debate the status of Germanic peoples from the rest of East Europe and increasingly treat Turks and refugees as undesirable aliens. If the numbers of East Germans requiring jobs and homes should rise to six-figure levels in the next year or so, interest in resettling Germans from socialist countries like the U.S.S.R. and Poland could wane further.

"In Kasakhstan," one lady told me, "they called us 'fascist Germans.' Now we're finally here in our homeland, and our children come home from school crying because their classmates had been calling them 'communist Russians.'"

Other resettlement problems plague the *Aussiedler*. The Mennonites among them, for instance, find the life and worship style of their fellows in the Federal Republic to be shockingly liberal and worldly, and have therefore, for the most part, chosen to establish their own congregations that preserve the conservative values they established in the U.S.S.R. Most of the immigrants express a similar reaction to liberal lifestyles in general, and most people agree that the generations react differently. The older folk tend to isolate themselves from modern influences, while the younger generation seeks to immerse itself in the milieu their parents reject. This is apparent in the families whose children have had five to ten years of German schooling and cultural influence. As a desperate defense against the perceived loss of values, one group of *Aussiedler* has established a large private school near Lage. More such developments are probable.

Before 1939, at least 9 million people of Germanic background lived in the eastern provinces of Germany; East Brandenburg, Pomerania, East Prussia and Upper and Lower Silesia were incorporated into the new Polish borders after World War II. Another 8.5 million were living in other Eastern European countries, often in German-speaking settlements. Both world wars forced the relocation of some of these people, primarily from countries that were at war with Germany.

The Mennonites, who make up between 10 and 15 percent of those *Aussiedler* currently returning from the U.S.S.R., are an example of ethnic Germans' tragic experience in East Europe. A radical Reformation group, the Mennonites were persecuted through the 16th, 17th and 18th centuries for their challenge to the state church represented by their rebaptism of adults based on faith alone. They were persecuted also for their refusal to bear arms, a tenet that subjected them to public ridicule and rejection as well as to the whims of rulers. A large number of this sect from the lowlands of North Europe sought freedom from the draft by moving to Prussia (now North Poland) and later, by invitation of Catherine the Great, to the Black Sea region of the Ukraine along the Dnieper River. Here they built up successful German-speaking agrarian and industrial colonies, and enjoyed considerable rights in self-government and religious practice through the 19th century. Several migrations to the Americas were organized be-

tween 1870 and 1900. Those that remained to face the October
Revolution of 1917 and its aftershocks experienced the full
horrors of the revolution's wrathful vengeance on the "Kulaks,"
the capitalists living off the fat of the land and the "labors of
the peasantry." Another series of migrations to the Americas
took place in the 1920s. The 50,000 or so who remained in
Eastern Europe endured imprisonment, starvation and repression.

In 1941, those remaining in the Black Sea area were seen as
potential German collaborators and were forcibly evacuated to
Siberia, where men and women alike were placed in forest and
mining labor camps. Many died there; others were drafted into
the army and died in the war between Stalin and Hitler. (One
man told me he fought in the Russian army and was taken prisoner by the Germans, and then was drafted into the German
army and taken prisoner by the Russians.) Some survived and
eventually settled down to reasonably stable living in places like
Karaganda, Alma-Ata, Dschambul and Frunze. Through it all,
their eyes wandered westward, to places like Canada or Paraguay
where virtually all had relatives by now, or to Germany where
people like Chancellors Willy Brandt and Helmut Schmidt repeatedly placed the dilemma of the East Europe Germans on the
table at Soviet-German discussions.

Glasnost, perestroika and Mikhail Gorbachev suddenly opened
the doors. For many it was an answer to prayer—and a dilemma.
Church-centered communities of Mennonites began to enjoy new
freedoms of religion and worship just as their ranks began to
disintegrate from emigration fever. Families with no relatives in
West Germany found themselves virtually alone, unable to obtain
exit visas while friends and neighbors frantically prepared to
leave. Churches gradually emptied, in some cases with unopened
boxes of recently shipped German Bibles stacked in corners. And
everyone who had the choice of leaving wrestled with the questions, How can we go and leave our parents (or married children)
behind? How can we go now that things are getting better? Can
we risk another Stalin?

For thousands of people of German descent in Eastern Europe, the decision has been obvious. History has taught them that
they will never be secure where they are, and that in Poland,
the U.S.S.R. or in Romania their very "Germanness" marks them.
For many, migration fulfills a dream nurtured for generations

through the hardships of the revolution, of the wars and of Stalinism.

But reality is often a poor respecter of dreams, and the open arms of the "homeland" are now beginning to close. An *Umsiedler* friend of mine endures a constant flow of anti-resettler sentiment from the woman whose house she cleans. "Write your relatives and friends back in the U.S.S.R. and tell them they won't like it here—they should stay at home," her employer tells her. "You people ruin the workplace for us first by taking our jobs away and then by working so hard and doing whatever you're told so employers play you off against the union and we all have to work harder."

My friend is so fed up with these narrow interpretations and prejudices that she insists she would quit if more respectable work were available. A few days ago, though, she found a way to respond to the lady's tirade: "We could understand why the Russians vented their hatred on us. We knew what Hitler and our fellow Germans had done to them. And so we learned to forgive them for mistreating us. And I expect we'll learn to forgive our detractors here in Germany as well."

Her husband, Jake, told me how one day when he was ten years old two teachers in his little schoolhouse in the Urals kept him after class and berated him in turn for neglecting his homework. "There's only one reasonable thing for you fascist brats," one said to him, "and that's to bury you alive in a barrel!"

The migration of the Germans back to their homeland may be an answer to prayer for people like Jake and his wife. But the rising hostility at their homecoming is something for which they hadn't planned.

UNIFICATION UNSETTLING FOR SOME
GERMAN JEWS[4]

On November 9, 1990, three buses waited at the Jewish Community Center in the western section of a freshly united Berlin to

[4]Article by John Schmidt, staff writer, from *Christian Century* 108:508–9 My 8 '91. Copyright 1991 by Christian Century Foundation. Reprinted by permission.

carry exquisitely dressed Jews and non-Jews to eastern Berlin's only synagogue. For the first time since 1961, Jews from both sides of Berlin would be marking the anniversary of the November 1938 pogrom together. On November 9 the Gestapo orchestrated a campaign of terror all over the country. Synagogues were burned, Jewish shops were smashed and looted, innocent Jews were arrested and transported to concentration camps. Between 150 and 200 Jews were killed during that night and the following day. The Nazis maintained that a spontaneous act of revenge against Jewish people had taken place. The Jews on the bus did not want this date to pass without appropriate observation. Skepticism and doubt filled the air, however, as the bus wound its way through the city. Would Germans choose to celebrate November 1989, the opening of the Berlin Wall, and ignore November 1938, or would the day echo simultaneously the highs and lows of German culture?

At the synagogue, Rita Sussmuth, president of the Bundestag, spoke about the Holocaust and Germany's commitment to bear responsibility for it, even as the separate states raced toward complete unification. Despite these assurances, East German Jews found themselves facing unsettling political and religious issues.

Peter Kirchner, who as a child had escaped from Berlin before the Gestapo had declared it *Judenrein* (free of Jews), served as the director of East Berlin's Jewish community until the final day of 1990. He seemed to embody the misgivings that East German Jews felt about religious and political unification. Kirchner had returned to East Germany after the war and stayed because it seemed to offer a safer haven for persecuted Jews than did West Germany. Although Kirchner never accepted the official East German dictate that anti-Semitism had been stamped out, he did recognize that East German Jews did not employ elaborate security systems or bullet-proof automobiles as did their brothers and sisters in West Berlin.

Now as his country folded he faced some disquieting prospects. "Now we belong to the Federal Republic of Germany, something we did not want," he said. "The individual was never given the opportunity to make a decision on the matter." In addition, plans were being made for the "takeover" of his Jewish community by the West Berlin Jews. Unification was not taking place on a political level alone: political unification had forced the religious communities into action, at times making East German Jews feel powerless. Despite the fact that the November observance was to take place in his own synagogue, Kirchner had received an invitation from the West Berlin offices only the day before the event. "I don't know what to think. Am I even wanted in my own community?"

Kirchner had cultivated a tiny survivors' community by emphasizing Jewish cultural and political programs. He was proud of the group of 135 practicing Jews who were more "politically astute" than the "keep smiling" community in West Berlin. Kirchner also prided himself on protecting the group from foreign pressures. When a group of American Jews wanted to help rebuild East Berlin's foremost synagogues, which had been destroyed not in 1938 but during an allied air attack on Berlin, Kirchner rejected the offer because it required that a plaque be erected in honor of the foreigners' contribution. Kirchner's critics contend, however, that he was not as successful in maintaining the integrity of the East Berlin community in its relationship to the state. Some claim that he had collaborated with the state, others that he had not demanded that the country's leader, Erich Honecker, address issues pertinent to Judaism. Kirchner argued that before unification, the 250 practicing Jews were hardly in the position to resist the government. East German Jews never enjoyed the political leverage or the wealth of West German Jews, but they found solace in one another, perhaps because of their small numbers.

Jewish questions were never addressed by East Germany until 1988, the 50th anniversary of the pogrom, and responsibility for the Holocaust was accepted only after unification had become a moot point. Incredibly, an autobahn scheduled to run directly through the heart of Europe's largest Jewish cemetery in Weissensee, a district of East Berlin, was diverted only after Heinz Galinski, director of West Berlin's Jews, intervened. The Holocaust as a Jewish event was largely ignored by East German historians. Jews were acknowledged to be victims of Nazi terror, but only inasmuch as the communists, trade unionists or homosexuals were. Like these other groups, Jews were "victims of fascism."

Conversely, West Berlin's politically conservative Galinski, who now heads the Jewish community of the united Berlin, enjoyed being the conscience of the West German state. He often held audience with high-ranking politicians and frequently questioned national and local policies. He wanted to open his community to the non-Jewish public to prevent past mistakes. To that end he hired Gad Beck to direct the educational program of the Jewish community in West Berlin in the 1970s and to establish a new focus for the center. Galinski, who last saw his parents, sister, wife and child at the selection ramp at Auschwitz, wanted to make the Jewish community transparent to German society in order to open dialogue, avoid misunderstandings and prevent harmful stereotypes. Beck's school soon had 97 percent non-Jewish participation.

The West Berlin community of 6,000 Jews (54 percent are from the Soviet Union) was widely respected and consulted. As a result, Beck's views on German unification are very different from Kirchner's. Beck sees the Jewish community, particularly with the influx of Jews from the Soviet Union, blossoming along with Berlin. Beck is, in fact, more concerned for the safety of other minorities than for the safety of Jews. He agrees with a young fascist who once told him: "If another Holocaust happens, all you Jews need to do is board El Al and fly to Israel."

Beck is concerned, however, with the West German economy's capacity to take over flagging East European businesses: "That's what I'm afraid of and that's got nothing to do with Jews." Beck claims that the current German economic might is comparable to the German industry which moved into Eastern Europe at the beginning of the 20th century. It also resembles, he contends, the expansionism of the Third Reich. Beck is not, however, overly concerned with the implications of German unification and is hesitant to condemn it. Some Jewish publications have written that a Jewish condemnation of German unification would only unleash an extremist anti-Semitic backlash.

Kirchner, on the other hand, is concerned with an actual upsurge in anti-Semitic activities, something previously unknown in East Germany. Recently Jewish politicians such as Gregor Gysi have faced anti-Semitic slogans. The grave of Bertolt Brecht (not a Jew) was smeared with the words "*Sau Jude raus!*" (Pig Jew out!) A monument to the 55,000 Berlin Jews exterminated in the Holocaust was recently overturned. And extreme rightist groups have, for the first time, begun to meet officially in eastern Germany. "We've never had to worry about that potential in our country before. My only hope is that we in Germany, through democratic processes, can reduce the threat which these groups represent," said Kirchner.

Kirchner's view of German unification is considerably bleaker than Galinski's or Beck's. He is facing religious and political structures completely unfamiliar to him, the loss of the distinct character of the East Berlin Jewish community, and, like so many millions, unemployment. Despite their differences, however, Jews both east and west feel compelled to remind the new German nation of the past.

III. THE DISMANTLING OF THE OLD REGIME IN EAST GERMANY

EDITOR'S INTRODUCTION

Even as the date of unification approached, the Communist regime in East Germany was undergoing rapid changes, leading to its dissolution. An entire bureaucracy found itself out of work and on the unemployment line. The issue of occupation by Russian troops was ultimately settled in the agreement between the new Germany and the Soviets, whereby the Russian forces would be withdrawn over the course of the next several years. This agreement, however, was costly to a united Germany, which agreed to pay vast sums to repatriate the 400,000 troops, and to provide for new housing for them on their return to the U.S.S.R. The dismantling of the East German state also involved disbanding the National People's Army and the Ministry for State Security, the vast secret police establishment known as *Staatsicherheit* or Stasi.

Writing in *U.S. News & World Report*, Robin Knight reports on the dissolution of East Germany's National People's Army, made up of 175,000 troops. Some will be absorbed into united Germany's forces, but no NPA veterans may become senior officers, and all will go through a rigorous retraining program. At the same time, the "two-plus-four" treaty between the two Germanys and the main World War II allies provides that no U.S. or non-German NATO forces will be deployed in East Germany. The second article, by Robert Darnton in *The New Republic*, discusses the storming of the Stasi headquarters on January 15, 1990 by a crowd of 100,000 East Germans.

A final article, by Bob Tedeschi in *Women's Sports and Fitness*, touches on another aspect of the dismantling of the East German system—its highly-touted athletic program that has earned their athletes 192 gold medals in Olympic competition since 1968. As Tedeschi points out, the state-funded system ran 23 children's sports schools, training athletically talented children single-mindedly in an effort to show off the "success" of the Communist regime. In the new system of private enterprise, however, the grooming of athletes in Germany will undergo many changes.

TAPS FOR AN UNLOVED EAST GERMAN ARMY[1]

The goose step is gone. So is the loyalty oath to the Communist state and vainglorious military decorations named after Marx and Lenin. Soldiers are even selling their uniforms to souvenir-hunting West German tourists. But the final humiliation for East Germany's National People's Army [NPA] is yet to come.

That will occur on October 3 [1990]—unification day—when the West German flag will be run up at all NPA barracks, the old uniforms will be thrown out and former East German soldiers will start wearing anonymous fatigues. West German officers will bring what remains of the NPA under Bonn's command. For an Army whose only significant action was to take part in the Soviet-led invasion of Czechoslovakia in 1968, it seems a particularly fitting, if abject, finale.

Given the scale and scope of West Germany's takeover of the East, it could not be otherwise. Except for the Communist Party and the secret police, no East German institution more faithfully served Kremlin interests. All officers had to be party members, tactics were honed to Soviet needs, and all equipment was Soviet-made. From the moment unification became a possibility, Bonn's military chiefs made it clear there was no future in the new Germany for such a force, which once numbered 175,000.

Ensuring loyalty. Fewer than 50,000 of the NPA's 90,000 current troops will be integrated into united Germany's 370,000-strong armed forces, a level set by recently signed treaties that restore German sovereignty for the first time since World War II. West Germany's active-duty military forces now total about 450,000. No NPA survivors will be senior officers, and all will go through a rigorous retraining program—similar to the de-

---

[1]Article by Robin Knight, staff writer, from *U.S. News & World Report* 109:48 O 1 '90. Copyright October 1, 1990 *U.S. News & World Report*. Reprinted by permission.

nazification drive which followed the establishment of the Bundeswehr in 1955—to ensure loyalty and suitability.

For the NPA's remaining 300 or so generals (63 already have been sacked by the non-Communist East German government), nothing lies ahead except retirement and a small pension. Younger officers must make do with even less: Welfare payments while they seek new jobs. Many NPA junior officers and enlisted men are reported to be trying to join the French Foreign Legion.

Dealing with disgruntled East German officers will be one of the easier tasks ahead. Far more complicated will be developing a strategy to defend what is now East German territory and disposing of mountains of unwanted Soviet-made equipment.

Under the two-plus-four treaty between the two Germanys and the main World War II Allies [the U.S., Great Britain, France, and the Soviet Union], no U.S. or non-German NATO troops will be deployed on former East German territory following unification. There will be no restrictions on stationing German troops there. Some 50,000 soldiers will be based in the old East Germany, says West German Defense Minister Gerhard Stoltenberg. But no more than 20,000 will be from the NPA, and entire Bundeswehr units may be transferred to the East.

Trying to integrate American, West European and Soviet-made weaponry would be a logistical nightmare. "We have no use for Soviet equipment in our armed forces," says a West German officer. "The Soviets can have it back and we may even pay them for it."

That may be more easily said than done. In its final days, the East German government fulfilled contracts with Moscow to buy $600 million worth of new equipment, including helicopter gunships, reinforced armor for T-72 tanks, guided missiles for armored personnel carriers, rocket launchers and ammunition. Bonn would like to hand back everything it can to the Soviets. Moscow is reluctant to accept such materiel, however, because under the terms of arms-control treaties now being negotiated, it would have to pay the $100 million or more cost of destroying the equipment. Breaking up a single main battle tank can cost $36,000, and the NPA has 2,200 of them. Much of the NPA's high-tech hardware, such as 22 MiG-29 fighters and 313 other combat aircraft, is unsalable because Soviet military personnel have stripped the communications gear and missile launching systems.

Despite the bleak outlook, some senior NPA commanders still

are seeking a role in the new Germany. In late August, the Navy's chief of staff, Adm. Hendrik Born, urged that 50 East German vessels join a unified Navy as a coastal-protection force. Bundesmarine officers ignored his pleas, citing "electronic incompatibility."

For an army that prided itself on its Prussian heritage, iron discipline and subordination to the civilian elite, the deepest wound may be popular disdain as the NPA passes into history. "People are totally indifferent to its fate," says an East German diplomat. "There are so many other things to worry about. No one is mourning its passing."

STASI BESIEGED[2]

Was January 15 another storming of the Bastille? The images left over from the bicentennial celebrations of the French Revolution are fresh enough for one to see it that way, but January 15 was no July 14 for the East Berliners. The crowd that stormed the headquarters of the Stasi [short for *Staatsicherheit*, Ministry for State Security] in the Ruchestrasse did not bring down a regime or string up any victims. It went on a romp, kicking through doorways and trashing furniture. Worse has occurred in American college panty raids, not to mention English soccer games.

But the East German government was shaken to its core. In a nationwide appeal, broadcast over television and radio, it sounded as though the country were on the brink of civil war. "The democracy that is just beginning to develop is in great danger," the statement warned. "The government of the German Democratic Republic appeals to all citizens in this critical hour to stay calm and collected." The government and the opposition parties broke off their negotiations at the Round Table, which is setting the political agenda until the May elections, and Prime Minister Hans Modrow rushed off to the Ruchestrasse as if he were determined not to botch things in the style of Louis XVI. "Is this a

[2]Article by Robert Darnton, professor of history at Princeton University, from *The New Republic* 202:15–16 18–19 F 12 '90. Copyright © 1990 by *The New Republic*. Reprinted by permission.

riot?" the king reportedly said on July 15, 1789. "No sire, a revolution," was the famous reply. Modrow seems to have feared a revolution and to have found a riot.

But his fears were not completely groundless. The first round of price increases—children's clothing, up 50 percent to 150 percent—had just taken place, producing mob scenes in department stores. The first important strike—a 24-hour stoppage by milk deliverers in Berlin—had just been announced. Immigration to West Germany continued unabated at a rate of more than 1,000 persons a day. And above all, the political situation began to boil.

Since the first of the year Modrow's government had made it clear that it meant to govern. It announced new measures without consulting the 16 opposition groups gathered at the Round Table. It refused the opposition parties' demands for equal access to offices, telephones, printing presses, automobiles, and television time, which have all been monopolized by the Communist (SED) Party. It rejected demands for a law on joint ventures, which would permit foreign firms to acquire controlling interests in East German enterprises. And it refused to budge on the Stasi issue.

The Stasi occupy a key place in the new political consciousness of the East Germans. In a lecture tour of university towns in the GDR from January 11 to 17, I found the obsession with the Stasi to be as pervasive as the push for unification. Every city has its Stasi citadel, a bastion surrounded by walls and covered with a forest of radio antennas. Every citizen has a collection of Stasi stories, which explain why he was not promoted or allowed to travel or admitted to an educational institution. A Stasi mythology about tapped telephones, steamed-open letters, and denunciations by domestic spies has spread throughout the country.

How much truth is there to it? No one could say before last November, when the Stasi stations were occupied by demonstrators and placed under the surveillance of Citizens' Committees. After a quick look through the secret files, mainly their own, committee members decided to keep the files sealed. To release the information, they announced, would be to set off endless feuds among people who had been denounced by their neighbors or betrayed by their spouses. Since the government had promised that the Stasi would be disbanded, it seemed that the myth could be allowed to dissipate in tavern talk.

But in December the government mounted a campaign for the suppression of neo-fascism, and the political spectrum began to change. Some Nazi-like graffiti had appeared on walls; some anti-Semitic remarks had been overheard in pubs; some Soviet memorials had been defaced; and a strong nationalistic current had surfaced in the opposition demonstrations, which have continued to take place in many cities, especially Leipzig.

How serious is this danger? The first alarm came from the opposition groups—a poorly organized and badly splintered coalition of parties and civic organizations that have only one thing in common: hostility to the SED. Nationalists had shouted down some New Forum speakers in the Leipzig demonstration of December 11, and it looked as though a new right might attempt to seize the anti-government movement from the hands of the new left, capitalizing on popular pressure for union with West Germany.

By early January, however, most of the left opposition groups, New Forum included, had endorsed unification in some form or other, usually with guarantees of the current borders and a proviso for the sanction of the major powers. Flag-waving is no longer a monopoly of the right, and the flag one sees everywhere—in demonstrations and even draped from apartment windows—is the flag of the Federal Republic. As East German intellectuals now describe it, neo-Nazism amounts to little more than spray-painting by teenagers, who get the greatest possible shock value in their protest against the regime by playing with the most powerful taboos in the regime's official culture: the symbols and slogans from the Hitler period. There is nothing except frustration behind the occasional swastika on the wall—no broad public support, no party, no Führer. The far right does not exist as an organized force essentially because the government has not permitted the radical Republican Party from West Germany to establish a foothold in the East.

The lack of dominant personalities, in the government as well as the opposition, makes East German politics look very different from those of Poland and Czechoslovakia, where personality cults have formed around Lech Walesa and Vaclav Havel. Gregor Gysi, the new leader of the SED, looks and sounds like an intellectual. As a defense lawyer, he developed a strong record of defending dissidents. And as Party secretary, he is known for his wit. He may be the only politician in either Germany with a sense of humor. No one could be less like a Hitler or a Stalin.

Yet the most common graffiti and demonstration banners now

say things like "Gysi-Stasi-Nasi" and "GyStasi." Instead of playing
with neo-nationalism, the opposition is trying to brand the regime
with the charge of "Stasinismus," i.e., with attempting to recon-
struct a police state. It began whipping up Stasi-consciousness,
and in doing so it provided the spark that set off the riot of
January 15.

The opposition groups adopted this strategy in response to a
government line, which went roughly as follows: neo-fascism is a
genuine threat; the public should rally to the government's struggle against it; to win the struggle, the government will have to
take strong measures; and strong measures can only be effective
by means of a security police, or "Verfassungsschutz" (constitution
protection), in the language of the SED. To the opposition groups
sitting at the Round Table, constitution-protecting sounded sus-
piciously like Stasi-reviving, all the more so as the promised liqui-
dation of the Stasi seemed to have come to a halt. Was the danger
of neo-fascism a bluff, used to cover up the creation of a new
police state while the SED maintained its monopoly on the media
and the means required to run a political campaign? As soon as
the government sponsored the idea of the danger, the public
began to disbelieve it: such is the state of confidence in public
authority in the GDR.

On January 8 the opposition groups delivered an ultimatum
to the government: either Modrow would inform them about the
state of the Stasi—the number of agents, their activities, and the
progress of their dissolution—or they would break off all negotiations, producing political chaos only four months before the general election. Modrow had tried to keep his distance from the
Round Table, arguing that he had to concentrate on governing
the country and that he reported to parliament—that is, the old
Volkskammer, where there is no real opposition to the SED. But
when faced with the ultimatum, he caved in.

On January 15, the morning before the riot, he appeared
before the Round Table and asked to make peace. He promised
to abandon all plans for establishing a new security force before
the elections, and he asked his main adviser, Manfred Sauer, to
report on the Stasi. Sauer's report was astonishing, even to those
with a highly developed Stasi-consciousness. The force consisted
of 85,000 regular employees, of whom only 30,000 had been
dismissed; it also included 109,000 secret informers. That is, one
of every 80 persons in the country, whose population is about 16
million, worked for the Stasi. The surveillance involved 1,052

full-time specialists who tapped telephones, 2,100 who steamed open letters, and 5,000 who followed suspects. The force had doubled since 1980 and had set as its goal the perfection of an espionage network that would cover every citizen in the GDR.

The Stasi armory included 200,000 pistols, which were being turned over to the Ministry of the Interior; a huge fleet of cars, which would be sold to the public (the waiting time for a car is 15 years); and 3,000 telephone lines, which would be integrated into the public phone system (only one of every three households has a telephone). In short, the Sauer report confirmed the wildest fantasies of the Stasi alarmists. The hundreds of Stasi officers collectively constituted a forbidden city, with its own barbers and grocers and sports facilities as well as an information apparatus that could reach into everyone's life and that no one from the outside had ever penetrated—not until January 15, 1990.

At 5 p.m. that afternoon, a crowd of about 100,000 gathered at the central Stasi office in Berlin for a demonstration organized by New Forum under the slogan "Imagination against Stasi and Nasi [sic]." The Sauer report made it unnecessary for them to use their imagination. Shouting "We are the people," they climbed a wall, forced open a door, and went on a rampage. They smashed furniture, urinated against walls, and painted graffiti such as "Never again Stasi" and "Down with the SED."

The damage was actually far less than the million marks announced by the government, but far more, psychologically, than the government can afford. For the first time since the beginning of their revolution, the Germans have resorted to violence. They have sacked the most feared fortress in the land, before television cameras, which carried the scene into households everywhere. They have stripped the secrecy off the old police state and shown it for what it was, an insidious network of corruption and denunciation woven into the core of the Communist Party. And they have transformed the political situation by exposing the Party's fragile hold on power.

"WHO RULES THIS COUNTRY TODAY?" was the headline on the Party newspaper in Halle on June 16. Modrow and the ministers? The Round Table? Or nobody? East Germany is drifting into dangerous waters, but this first shot of violence seems to have charged people with new energy. "Germans are supposed to obey orders, not to defy them," a young man in Halle explained. He cited the old saw: There will never be a revolution in Germany, because before storming the train stations the Germans will queue up to buy platform tickets. "We are having a revolution," he said proudly. "And we have stormed the Stasi."

THE HIGH PRICE OF FREEDOM[3]

In the summer of 1989, Sybilli Schimmel's life was traveling along as if it were on autopilot. After all, the routine had been the same for years. An eight-year veteran of the East German women's handball team, Schimmel would rise early in the morning in her one-bedroom apartment in East Berlin, have a bite to eat, then climb into her exhaust-spewing Trabant automobile for the 10-minute ride to her sports club.

There, she would spend the entire day practicing with the team, lifting weights, running and listening to coaching lectures. At some point in the day Schimmel would also find herself flushing down the toilet the steroids that were routinely given to her by the coaching staff. It was business as usual for an East German athlete.

But even as that summer progressed, there were signs that Schimmel's autopilot life would change. The hushed voices of political dissenters grew in volume. And when autumn settled and the people gathered in the streets, demanding the end of communist rule, Schimmel and all her fellow East Germans decided to take control of the stick, and shut off the autopilot button for good.

"I have a whole new existence now," says 26-year-old Schimmel, in a room in her new sport club in West Berlin. "I have more money, a new car—no 'Trabby' anymore—and a new apartment [in West Berlin] with two bedrooms. A new existence of Sybilli Schimmel has begun."

It's telling that Schimmel defines her new life by discussing the basic changes in lifestyle rather than her athletic career. For years, East Germany showcased its athletes as the primary successes in a "successful" political system, only to neglect the everyday needs of its citizens. Now, as is the case with Schimmel, democracy seems

[3]Article by Bob Tedeschi, staff writer, from *Women's Sports & Fitness* p44–50 J/F '91. Copyright 1991 by *Women's Sports & Fitness*. Reprinted by permission.

destined to care for those needs. As for sports—and women's sports in particular—however, the story is different. With children's sports schools closing, private sponsorships for most women's sports lagging and state funding for athletes diminishing, women's sports in a unified Germany face the unenviable task of living up to their lofty reputation without many of the factors that made that reputation possible.

As a member of the East German women's handball team, Schimmel's work was always a bit more strenuous than that of the other members of the socialist society, but it was also much more rewarding. In exchange for their athletic talent, women athletes were given educations in the nation's elite sports schools, a salary that was at least 50 percent higher than the average East German (often paid by the army or secret police, of which many athletes were ostensibly members), and monetary and material incentives for superior achievement in international competitions. The opportunities to travel throughout the world, too, were luxuries that only a handful of East Germans were permitted.

It was the promise of such luxuries that had attracted thousands of women to athletic careers ever since East Germany decided to use sports as a vehicle for promoting communism in the mid-60s. As long as the medals continued to roll in, they were told, the government would provide.

And roll they did. Since their first Olympic competition as an individual national team in 1968, East German athletes have won 192 gold medals. East German women garnered 95 of those golds. For a country with a population about equal to that of New York state (roughly 17 million), the results were staggering.

How did they do it? First of all, the East Germans had a plan. Knowing they had limited funds to work with, the government chose to promote sports that could return the most medals for every dollar invested. Thus, the so-called "medal-maximum" sports, such as swimming, track and field, luge and rowing, were given the most money. In these sports, not only could one superb athlete win several medals, but the athlete's training and equipment costs were relatively paltry. Team sports that could only garner one medal and that required more equipment and staff support, meanwhile, were virtually cut off from funding.

Women's athletics, on the other hand, were viewed as a veritable gold mine of "medal-maximum" sports, primarily because women's sports had yet to be brought into the era of modern training. "It was easier [to win medals] in a discipline like women's track and field than in men's track and field, in which training had already been very [serious] for a long time," says Norbert Skowronek, the executive director of the Berlin Sports Federation.

And because the East German women were the first to jump headlong into extensive weight training and heavy aerobic training, they were able to develop more quickly and more completely than the women of other nations, who were still too leery of jeopardizing their femininity to experiment with such techniques.

"I remember the 1972 Olympics in Munich, there was a woman named Renate Stecher—a woman with such shoulders," says Skowronek, extending his hands beyond the width of his own shoulders. Stecher, the 100-meter and 200-meter Olympic champion in Munich "ran much faster than the other girls," he says. "To get such high quality you must train much more than the others."

To get such high quality, some would argue, you must also sometimes cheat. For years, the East German women were scrutinized for their oftentimes masculine appearance, while somehow always managing to pass drug tests. And although sports officials and athletes now acknowledge the widespread use of anabolic steroids, few are willing to speak openly about the extent to which such drugs were used.

"We didn't talk about it," says Sylvia Gerasch, a former world-record holder in the 100-meter breast-stroke, when asked about steroid use among her teammates. Gerasch, who admitted to taking steroids for a period two years before setting the world record, was reluctant to discuss the use of steroids among her teammates. "It was more an individual thing," she said. Schimmel, meanwhile, says all her teammates on the national handball team were given steroids by the coaching staff, but most chose to flush the steroids down the toilet, because they "did not want to look like men." She estimated, however, that 30 percent of the team did take drugs.

But neither steroids nor the incentive system nor the long hours of training could claim credit for the East German women's dominance of the '70s and '80s. Such credit belongs to two elements, according to the nation's sports leaders: an extensive system of finding and cultivating talent in the children's sports schools and the expertise and sheer numbers of coaches, trainers and sports scientists whose careers were devoted to athletic perfection.

Twenty-three children's sports schools were sprinkled throughout East Germany, each one catering to two or three different sports. Every child was tested for physical fitness and growth potential before he or she reached the age of eight and was either selected to go to a sports school or sent to regular school. The youngest children—most often gymnasts—would start at the sports schools at the age of 6, and all were paid a monthly salary from the age of 10.

Meanwhile, the supply of coaches at the schools and the training centers was inexhaustible. The East had about one coach for every three athletes (the ratio in the West is one to 20). Because the coaches in the East worked closely with some of the world's best sports scientists, the level of expertise among East German coaches was often superior to that of the West.

Buoyed by the successes of the system, fans in East Germany rallied around the athletes and coaches for years. But the support was not ironclad. As the '80s brought economic stagnation throughout the Eastern Bloc nations, the VIP status of elite athletes became increasingly vexing to the general populus. Last fall, therefore, when the public cried out for democratic reforms, changes in the sports system were high among the list of demands. A $500 million-per-year sports system could no longer pacify a public that lacked basic necessities.

When the West German government agreed to absorb the East into its economic and political system, the final nails were put into the coffin of the East German sports machine. "It was a perfect system in the GDR," says Karlheinz Gieseler, who was the executive director of the West German Sports Federation for 25 years until his retirement last December. "But you cannot bring it into a democratic system. A democratic sports system is entirely different from a socialist one."

The primary difference is money. Finding the kind of money needed to sustain the East German sports system after unification was out of the question. Since the spring of last year, when the East German sports authority came under the control of the West German Sports Federation, money has been scarce. For the second half of this year, the West German government gave $60 million to the East German sports authority, in effect saying, "Here you are, don't spend it all in one place. And for good measure, you can disband the army and secret service teams, too."

What are the results of this austerity? Gone are most, if not all, of the children's sports schools. Gone are at least 85 percent of the

4,000 East German coaches who were often hailed as the world's best. Gone are the Olympic training centers. Gone, too, are many of the athletes who dominated their sports—"To other countries," says Werner Neumann, one of five executive directors of the East German sports authority. "We haven't the money [to keep them]."

Because of the anemia of the East German economy, the money may not be there in the future, either. The fate of the coaches, athletes and training centers is intrinsically linked to that of the East German economy, the prognosis of which is about as good as that of lasting peace in the Middle East. Nearly half of the nation's work force of nine million will be out of work by the spring of '91, economists say, as industries expected to invest in eastern Germany are balking.

Without a strong economy, the one thing that keeps a democratic sports system thriving—private sponsorship—is absent. When asked about the sponsorship possibilities for sports after unification, Neumann was exasperated. "We're coming from the Middle Ages here," says Neumann, adding, "Who is sponsoring a country that's going down?"

More important, perhaps is the question "who wants to sponsor sports that no one wants to watch?" When it comes to finding sponsors, women's sports in particular face a bleak future. East German sponsors and television stations have traditionally been interested in a woman athlete's looks just as much as—if not more than—her athletic performances. Because East German women have often forsaken femininity for medals, sponsors could be reluctant. "Most of the GDR girls were not a sight we'd describe as beautiful," says Skowronek. "So only from time to time will there be a chance for sponsorships."

One notable exception is Katarina Witt, the East German figure skater who captured gold medals at the '84 and '88 Olympics. But Witt has spoken out in defense of the old system, saying that sports in East Germany will "go a little down the ladder now."

The only survivor of the system could be women's track and field, which has so far been able to attract enough sponsors to remain strong. But even this East German sports mainstay could suffer from the same maladies as other sports. A spokesman for the largest TV network in West Germany says, "[East German] sports are not interesting to audiences or TV companies." With coaches leaving the country in droves and the sports schools closing, experts predict the East Germans can stay competitive only until the Barcelona Olympic Games in '92. Beyond that, they say, sponsors and TV stations won't even offer a fleeting glance at the East.

In the face of all this bleakness, however, are rays of sunlight. First, drugs will not be nearly as prevalent in a unified German sports system, because the West Germans have strict penalties for drug use and require regular testing. Plus, elite athletes will have to play by the same rules as the general populus when it comes to pool time or track time. Perhaps most important, eastern Germany will enter a new era in which mass sports take precedence over elite sports. Programs are already being developed to induce participation in mass sports activities throughout eastern Germany's five states, and the German Sports Federation is offering monetary incentives to those in the East who want to run private sports clubs that include mass sports programs.

There may also be a glimmer of hope for elite sports in eastern Germany. There are those in the West German Sports Federation who are pushing to retain some of the sports schools and coaches after unification. According to Norbert Wolf, the federation's executive director, the government is reviewing a '91 budget request of $200 million—double what it received last year. But with the eastern German population less than one-third of the west's, there is expected to be resistance—if not outright disdain—for the idea. Says Jurgen Aretz, a spokesman for the Ministry of Intra-German Affairs, "Sports will change [in the east] by making it possible for normal people to get involved. Top athletes will find ways anyway."

If spectator interest in East German sports is any indication, bureaucrats like Aretz could be justified in letting the entire East German sports system die. Bernd State, a press officer for the East German sports authority, sat in the stands at the recent East German Track and Field Championships in Dresden, shaking his head in dismay. The stadium, usually filled to capacity with screaming fans, was nearly empty as the finals of the women's 100-meter sprint got underway.

"Our view is much wider than before," he said, his hands forming a bracket around an imaginary horizon. "Now [instead of coming here], people are going to the other countries, visiting friends they couldn't meet before. People have many more possibilities to do all the things they couldn't before."

And in this region, where the people are still getting accustomed to having total control over their own lives, even those

with a connection to East Germany's sports glory years understand that they must take a back seat. "You can't blame them," says
Neumann of those who are dismantling eastern Germany's sports
system. "There are more important things than sports at the moment. People are free now to do what they like."

IV. A UNITED GERMANY: OUTLOOK FOR THE FUTURE

EDITOR'S INTRODUCTION

This section brings together articles that consider the future of a united Germany. The first, written by Otto Friedrich for *Time*, provides a good deal of historical background and raises the question of how much there is to fear from a united Germany, especially in the light of its militarist past from Bismark to Hitler. Rejecting the notion of an inflexible and unchanging national character, Friedrich does not feel that the world need stand in fear of Germany today. Josef Joffe in *Commentary* reaches similar conclusions. Conditions that led to a militarist nationalism, he remarks, do not now exist; rather, conditions favor a Germany that succeeds through economic preeminence within the structure of a European security system.

The next two articles present opposing views of Germany's future. Writing in *The New Republic*, Niall Ferguson argues that Germany in the future will be both less nationalistic and less economically powerful than it had been formerly, with the cost of unifying the country keeping the country in debt for at least the next decade. However, Douglas Stanglin, in a *U.S. News & World Report* article, forsees a Germany so powerful economically that it could break free of European Community restraints and dominate all of Europe. The final article, by Angela Stent in *Foreign Policy*, speculates on a new and powerful Germany's future relations with its European neighbors, the Soviet Union, and the United States.

GERMANY TOWARD UNITY[1]

The profound and icy mistrust which the German arouses whenever he gets any

[1]Article by Otto Friedrich, staffwriter, from *Time* 136:66–71 Jl 9 '90. Copyright 1990 The Time Inc. Magazine Company. Reprinted by permission.

power into his hands is the aftermath of that vast horrible fear with which, for long centuries, Europe dreaded the wrath of the Teutonic blond beast.
—FRIEDRICH NIETZSCHE

The 16 million citizens of East Germany will be $70 billion richer this week, at least on paper. Even before the day of reckoning this past Sunday, crowds had been standing patiently in line to complete the paper work for converting their ostmark savings into deutsche marks at a rate of 1 to 1 for up to 6,000 marks, and 2 to 1 for anything beyond that. On Sunday itself, cash was being handed out at some 10,000 bank branches, police stations and temporary disbursing points. The vast shift in wealth is part of the price of German unification.

As of that day of economic union between the Federal Republic and the German Democratic Republic, an entire society will be transformed. After nearly a half-century of communism, East Germans are now living under West German rules on corporate and union activities, welfare and insurance. Although there is still no agreement on important details of the political and military future, the economic merger reflects a historic moment that until recently few people imagined they would ever live to see: the peaceful rejoining of Germany. Before long, the united country will take West Germany's official name, the Federal Republic of Germany, and the G.D.R. will formally be abolished.

The merger process is not proving to be easy—and no one expected it to be. The most nettlesome outstanding issue is the military future of Central Europe, with Moscow balking at the West's insistence that a united Germany remain a full member of NATO. The West has offered substantial inducements: no NATO troops in East Germany, the continuance of Soviet forces there for a time at German expense, plus substantial German aid to the Soviet economy.

On the domestic side, questions remain on how to raise the East to the West's level of prosperity and how to smooth the joining of different economic and social systems. There are arguments about where the new capital should be: in the imperial—and Nazi—capital of Berlin or in democratic but provincial Bonn.

Whatever the obstacles, the conservative governments of Chancellor Helmut Kohl in Bonn and Prime Minister Lothar de Mazière in East Berlin are pressing full speed ahead. Kohl in particular is determined, as he puts it, "not to miss the unification train, which may not come another time." With a large majority in both Germanys supporting merger—even though there are some reservations as to speed and cost—the Chancellor is planning to hold all-German elections in early December.

All the economic problems can be negotiated among the Germans themselves, but among their neighbors, unification has aroused quite different concerns. Will a united Germany mean the rebirth of dreaded words like *Lebensraum* and *Drang nach Osten?* In short, will a united Germany turn nationalistic, threaten its neighbors and try to dominate Europe? "Today the Germans want to think of the future," says Fritz Stern, Seth Low professor of history at Columbia University, "but their neighbors are thinking of the past."

On the evidence of the past two or three decades, which is all the evidence needed on most other political questions, such anxieties seem almost irrational. Germany was mostly united back in 1949, when the U.S., British and French zones of military occupation—70% of Germany's 1945 territory and 72% of the nation's population—were merged to form the Federal Republic, with its headquarters in Bonn. Economically, the figures are even more impressive: the East German economy that now has been joined to that of West Germany forms only one-tenth of the combined total. During those past 40 years, the world witnessed cruel wars in Korea, Vietnam, Algeria, Lebanon, Afghanistan and Nicaragua, but the mostly united Germans caused no trouble to anyone.

Yet even their recent peacefulness can apparently be held against them. "The Federal Republic is unique among the great powers in [that] it came to life without a drop of blood being shed in its birth," Arthur Miller wrote in the New York *Times.* "No German soldier can say, 'I fought for democracy' . . . What Germans lack now is the consecration by blood of their democratic state . . . " But whose blood should the Germans have shed in their "consecration," and what would Miller say if any German were foolish enough to offer such a gory theory of "democratic faith"?

Part of this self-induced anxiety about German unification derives from the widespread but questionable theory that different nations have different national characters, that the Germans, because of their history or their upbringing or whatever, are both aggressive and docile, robot-like people who love order and discipline, work and war. Like the stereotypes of the snobbish English or the immoral French or the crass Americans, such caricatures are generally created by one's enemies, often in times of war.

"There is such a thing as national character, but it changes," says William Manchester, a Wesleyan University adjunct professor of history and author of *The Arms of Krupp.* "And the German national character has changed. The Germans are united by language, by culture. And young Germany—which is most of Germany today—is also united by a horror of the Second and Third Reichs."

The real origin of the suspicions about Germany's future is, of course, its dark past, namely the crimes committed during the twelve-year reign of Adolf Hitler. Hitler, after all, did not commit those crimes by himself; other Germans piloted the bombers over Warsaw, and other Germans operated the gas chambers at Auschwitz. Though the majority of today's Germans were not even born when those crimes were committed, the nation remains tainted by the Nazi legacy that endures in the world's memory.

While millions of people know about the horrors of Hitler's Third Reich, it seems all too widely forgotten that German history did not begin in 1933. Nor did it begin in 1871, when Bismarck created the autocratic Second Reich. German history goes back more than 2,000 years, to a murky era when a variety of Germanic tribes lived in a land that, according to [the Roman historian] Tacitus, "either bristles with forests or reeks with swamps." Even then, German tribesmen had a reputation as fearsome fighters, and it was immensely important to the future history of Europe that they annihilated three Roman legions in the Teutoburg Forest in A.D. 9, leaving the Rhine as the frontier between the Roman and Germanic worlds. But it was the Romans who originally invaded those forests to "pacify" the Germans, as they had pacified Gaul and Britain.

The Germanic tribes began moving into Roman territory during the 3rd century, not as the "barbarian" invaders of popular legend but as immigrants and refugees. Even the Visigoths, who conquered Rome in A.D. 410, subjecting it, in Gibbon's majestic words, to the "licentious fury of the tribes of Germany and Scythia," had originally entered the empire peacefully, and many had loyally served in the Roman army. The celebrated sacking of Rome was primarily a humiliation, nothing like the all-out Roman destruction of Carthage, Thebes and Jerusalem.

The idea of restoring the Roman empire three centuries later inspired Charlemagne to voyage to Rome in A.D. 800 and have himself crowned by the Pope. Both Germany and France claim the Frankish leader, for he governed from Aachen (Aix-la-Chapelle), and the territory under his rule rather closely resembled what is today the European Community. Not long after his death, however, his empire was divided among three grandsons.

While France and Britain developed centralized monarchies in the late Middle Ages, the German empire remained a crazy quilt of kingdoms, duchies, bishoprics, free cities and other flotsam. In the late 13th century, the imperial crown came into the hands of a Swiss family named Habsburg, but the Habsburgs' only real power and wealth came from their family possessions in Austria and Bohemia; the Germanic Holy Roman Empire, a concept that exercised a magic attraction in the Middle Ages, had about as much authority as the United Nations has today.

And then in 1517, the political divisions also became religious—and correspondingly bloodier. An obscure monk named Martin Luther nailed to the church door in Wittenberg his 95 theses against the Roman Church's sale of indulgences, partial pardons for souls in purgatory. The Lutheran faith, subsequently known as Protestantism, spread rapidly across northern Germany. Then, in the fratricidal ordeal known as the Thirty Years' War (1618–48), the French, Swedes and other nations joined in playing out their political and religious rivalries on German soil. Much of Germany was devastated and the starving survivors reduced to misery. In one of his best plays, *Mother Courage,* Bertolt Brecht sketched the scene: "The religious war has lasted 16 years, and Germany has lost half its inhabitants. Those who are spared in battle die by plague. Over once blooming countryside, hunger rages. Towns are burned down. Wolves prowl the empty streets . . ."

Gordon Craig, professor emeritus of history at Stanford University and author of *The Germans,* sums up this tragic period: "The Germans from earliest times were a free and independent people, and dreadful things happened to them, which inhibited those qualities and induced others. After the Thirty Years' War, habits of authoritarianism and dependence crept into the behavior of average Germans. One result is what one German writer has called the 'retarded nation.' The nation never did have the opportunity to get a political education, as in the English Enlightenment or the American Enlightenment."

The feebleness of the Habsburg suzerainty over fragmented Germany inspired not only the aggressiveness of France but also that of a newcomer—Prussia. Originally a Baltic tribe, the Prussians were conquered and Christianized in a 13th century "cru-

sade" by the Order of Teutonic Knights, but only in 1525 was the
remote duchy of Prussia acquired through a marriage by the
Hohenzollerns, the family that served as electors of Brandenburg. Brandenburg-Prussia was a rather bleak and impoverished
land, its capital, Berlin, little more than a dusty garrison town.
But its ruling Hohenzollern family was shrewd and single-mind-
ed in building up its wealth, its holdings and its army. When King
Frederick the Great acquired the throne in 1740, just as Maria
Theresa became Empress of Austria, he ruthlessly attacked her
and seized the prosperous province of Silesia. Maria Theresa
fought two bitter and unsuccessful wars of revenge, then shame-
lessly joined Prussia and Russia in partitioning Poland. Frederick
thus put together for the first time the various Hohenzollern
holdings from East Prussia to the Rhine.

Frederick's Prussia claimed with some justice to be a major
power in Europe, but his successors lacked his many talents, and
when the French once again appeared on the horizon, Prussia
ignominiously collapsed before Napoleon on the battlefield at
Jena. Napoleon finally abolished the moribund Holy Roman Empire in 1806, keeping the title Emperor for himself. He seized all
German territory west of the Elbe and created a French-domi-
nated Confederation of the Rhine, with his brother Jerome as
King of Westphalia. As Napoleon was retreating from Moscow in
1812, however, the repeatedly beaten Germans rose up again to
fight what they still call the Wars of Liberation. An allied army
defeated Napoleon at Leipzig, drove him back to Paris and then
into exile.

The Europe that was reconstituted at the Congress of Vienna
in 1815 included a new German Confederation, headed by the
Habsburgs of Austria, but also containing 38 other kingdoms,
duchies, free cities and such. It had a great culture—this was the
age of Beethoven and Schubert, Goethe and Hegel—but it was
hardly a nation. The very idea of German unification was nothing
more than an abstract concept, a dream of liberal intellectuals.

The last French invasion was the invasion of another idea:
revolution. When Paris mobs overthrew King Louis-Philippe in
1848, radicals and nationalists all over Europe took heart. The
Italians rose against their Habsburg overlords; and even in dormant Germany, crowds began marching through the streets of
Berlin, Vienna, Dresden. The armies of Germany's princes
eventually suppressed these demonstrations, but not before liber-
als organized a constituent assembly, which met in Frankfurt and
drafted an all-German constitution. The legislators decided that

they could put their ideas into practice only by offering the crown of a united Germany to King Frederick William IV of Prussia. But he considered himself King of Prussia by the grace of God, and scorned any crown offered him by people or parliament.

The members of the confederation still met in Frankfurt, and the Habsburg delegates still exerted unofficial leadership, but the young Prussian delegate determined that this must be changed. "Before very long," Bismarck wrote back to Berlin, 'we shall have to fight for our lives against Austria . . . because the progress of events in Germany has no other issue." Prussia's King William I appointed Bismarck Minister-President in 1862, and within four years, Bismarck was ready for a showdown with Austria. Prussia's chief of staff, Count Helmuth von Moltke, had revived the army of Frederick the Great, making it once again Europe's best. Moltke attacked the Austrians and cut them to pieces. Germany's three centuries of intermittent civil war between north and south, Protestant and Catholic, Hohenzollern and Habsburg, were now over.

Bismarck was convinced, and probably rightly, that France would never permit a united Germany, so he provoked Emperor Napoleon III into a misguided declaration of war. Moltke invaded France with 300,000 men, trapped the French at Sedan and captured the Emperor and 100,000 of his men. When an improvised government in Paris proclaimed the Third Republic and vowed to continue the war, Moltke insisted on besieging Paris. By now it seemed clear to the German princes who had followed Prussia into the war that their future lay in a united Germany under Prussian leadership. Bismarck artfully arranged to have William crowned Kaiser (Caesar) in January of 1871 in the palace of Versailles, that bastion of the French kings, while the hungry citizens of nearby Paris endured the Prussian siege.

For the next 20 years Bismarck used all his craft and guile to maintain the peace among Europe's constantly maneuvering rulers. But his Reich was deeply undemocratic: he despised the legislators of the Reichstag, and was not responsible to them, but only to the Kaiser, whom he bullied and cajoled. Everyone expected that when the aged William finally died, his relatively liberal and high-minded son Frederick would lead the empire into a more enlightened era. But when William did die, in 1888, Frederick was already mortally ill with throat cancer, and so the throne soon passed to his temperamental and bellicose son William II, then 29, of whom his own mother once said, "My son will be the ruin of Germany."

Unwilling to tolerate the domination of the 73-year-old Bismarck, William forced him out of office, took charge of military and diplomatic matters and left the rest to underlings. When a band of pro-Serbian nationalists assassinated the Austrian Crown Prince Ferdinand at Sarajevo in 1914, all the great powers found themselves enmeshed in a net of commitments that almost guaranteed disaster. The Austrians declared war on Serbia. The Russians went to the defense of their fellow Slavs and the Germans to that of the Austrians. When the French mobilized, the Germans declared war on them, and when the Germans invaded Belgium, the British honored a commitment to defend Belgian neutrality.

Historians of the day spent a good deal of effort trying to demonstrate German "war guilt," but in retrospect, it all seems more a tragedy of errors. The German strategy somewhat optimistically called for a bold sweep all the way to Paris and then an encirclement of the French defenders. But the French blocked the offensive at the Marne, within 30 miles of Paris. Then came the years-long horrors of trench warfare, with thousands of lives wasted for the capture of a few hundred feet of barbed wire and mud. Plus all the horrors that modern technology could add to the arts of combat: bombers, tanks, machine guns, poison gas. When it was over, four years later, more than 3 million German and Austro-Hungarians were dead, as well as 4.8 million of the Allies, including 126,000 Americans—not just numbers, but the best of a whole generation.

The German, Austrian and Russian empires disappeared. In Berlin the Socialists proclaimed from the balcony of the imperial palace the birth of what would be known to history as the Weimar Republic. Though still physically united—minus West Prussia, which was turned over to the newly independent Poland to give it a corridor to the sea—Germany was still divided against itself. Traditionalists in the army, business, the judiciary and the schools never believed in the republic at all. Right-wing extremists, including a young Austrian demagogue named Adolf Hitler, attempted coups in 1920 and 1923. Others sabotaged the political process by assassinations. A powerful Communist Party periodically staged strikes and street battles. The punitive peace treaty imposed at Versailles forced Germany to pay huge war damages. Out of that came the ruinous inflation of 1923, when the reichsmark plummeted to 4.2 trillion to the dollar, wiping out both the savings and the faith of the middle class.

Substantial U.S. aid helped the Weimar Republic in the late '20s. But it was a fragile recovery, overseen by a badly splintered

Reichstag and the octogenarian President Paul von Hindenburg, the losing commander in the war. When the Wall Street crash of 1929 set off a worldwide depression, Germany's new prosperity crumbled. The number of unemployed soared from 1.5 million to almost 2.5 million in just the month of January 1930.

And a new voice was heard in the land, shouting that this was all the fault of the "system," of foreigners and Jews. "Germany, awake!" cried Adolf Hitler, and a frightened, impoverished and traumatized people began to listen. In private, the neurotic Hitler had a different view: "Brutality is respected. The people need wholesome fear. They want to fear something. They want someone to frighten them and make them shudderingly submissive."

Hitler's National Socialist Party, which had only 17,000 members in 1926, metastasized to 120,000 in 1929, to 1 million in 1930. Wealthy industrialists began contributing handsomely. In the Reichstag, the Nazis held an insignificant twelve seats until the elections of 1930. By 1932 they had 230 seats, the largest bloc in the Reichstag.

Central to the question of what went wrong is the question of whether Hitler's rise to power was inevitable. Was there some fatal flaw in the history of Germany that predestined it to the swastika and the gas chamber? In one sense, everything that has happened may seem inevitable, simply because of the fact that it did happen. Yet it is extraordinary how narrowly Hitler triumphed, how many accidents and variables had to line up.

He still did not have a majority in 1932, and the constitution permitted President Hindenburg to name any Chancellor he wished, authorizing him to rule by a series of presidential decrees. The first time Hindenburg summoned Hitler and asked him to support a conservative regime headed by a dapper courtier named Franz von Papen, Hitler demanded full power for himself; Hindenburg not only refused but dressed Hitler down for lacking "chivalry." In the last pre-Hitler elections in November of 1932, the Nazis lost strength, from 230 seats to 196. The party was an estimated $5 million in debt, unable to pay the storm troopers who fought its street battles. "The future looks dark and gloomy," the Nazi party chief for Berlin, Joseph Goebbels, wrote in his diary at the start of 1933. "All chances and hopes have quite disappeared."

Then in the first week of January, chances and hopes almost miraculously returned. Hindenburg was persuaded to try the idea of a new conservative coalition: Hitler as Chancellor, Papen

as Vice Chancellor, with only two other Nazis in the Cabinet. "In
this way," said the non-Nazi Minister of Economic Affairs, "we will
box Hitler in." A fatal misjudgment. A month later, the Reichstag
was in flames, Hitler was persuading Hindenburg to suspend civil
liberties, and the most terrible chapter in 20th century history was
about to open.

So what is the lesson for 1990?

"There is no European country that hasn't had its moments of
trying to swallow up its neighbors, and I don't think Germany is
any worse than any other country," says Carl Schorske, Princeton
professor emeritus of history and author of *Fin de Siècle Vienna*.
"Since the war, Germany has become rather European. In fact,
even in the clues of personal behavior—the way people walk, the
way people greet you, the way they speak their language—in all
these things, there has been a tremendous change in Germany
since the Nazis. I don't see another Nazism on the horizon."

"Germany is not a fixed concept or entity," says Gordon Craig.
"It's something that has changed through the years. The history
of Germany has been a long, slow, disappointed voyage toward
the light, toward popular freedom. It started with the Enlightenment and was defeated. It tried to revive and was defeated by the
way Germany was united in 1871. Finally, thanks to the utter
destruction of Germany in 1945, it got another chance, and is
now being realized. We should be celebrating reunification with at
least two cheers."

"The Germans are being given a second chance," says Stern.
"That is the rarest of gifts, and one can only hope that they will do
justice to it. The Germans deserve friends who feel the burden of
the past, as so many of them do, but who have compassion for a
people who have had so rich and terrifying a history."

In Germany itself, there are still observers capable of taking
the future a little less seriously. One of the cleverest is the novelist
and critic Hans Magnus Enzensberger, whose latest book, *Europe,
Europe,* includes a scene in which an American reporter visits
Berlin in the year 2006. He finds himself in the midst of an
environmental conference being conducted in the traditional
Berlin style. "Masked demonstrators from the eco-anarchist milieu clashed with officers of the environmental police. A represen-
tative of the chemical industry, who made profuse ritual protesta-
tions of humility and reassurance, was shouted down." Going to
look at the onetime Berlin Wall, the reporter finds that it is now a
nature preserve. "A unique biotope," says an official. "There are

wild rabbits here, hedgehogs, opossums." The problem is that the environmentalists' efforts to get rid of the Wall are being blocked by art historians. "They regard the Wall as a work of art," the official complains, "because of the graffiti." An expatriated Scot finally explains to the American that the "famous reunification" back in the 1990s was "all just coffee and cakes." "Do you still remember how frightened of the Germans everyone was in the '90s? And what's happened? Nothing at all. Since then the German bogeyman has very quietly been laid to rest. We fell for it because we didn't know the first thing about German history."

ONE-AND-A-HALF CHEERS FOR GERMAN UNIFICATION[2]

Writing in the *International Herald Tribune,* a German Jewish journalist poured it all out. A "unified Germany," this son of Holocaust survivors warned, "may grow into everything the world abhorred in the Germany of the early part of the century: a powerful country never content to accept limits on its political or economic strength, a self-centered society . . . whose rulers remain happily oblivious to foreigners' concerns." The new Germany might resemble the "bizarre monarchy that was the Reich around the turn of the century." World War I followed, and then the doomed Weimar Republic, paving the "way for the rise of the Nazi party [and for a] government that made mass murder a main goal of its agenda." Soon, we might be watching the replay. "The peaceful and moderately dull Federal Republic of Germany . . . is leaving the stage. Its replacement, a rich and mighty entity, . . . may become a strange and eerie place—perhaps even the source of a new wave of darkness spreading over the earth."

This is the archetypal horror scenario that has haunted observers around the world since the Berlin Wall fell last November—Jews and non-Jews, Americans, Frenchmen, Britons, Russians, even Germans themselves. Nor is it so strange that people

[2]Article by Josef Joffe, author and the editor of *Suddeutsche Zeitung,* Munich, from *Commentary* 89:26–33 J '90. Copyright 1990 by *Commentary.* Reprinted by permission. All rights reserved.

should be oppressed by such dark visions of Germany *rediviva*.
Though Auschwitz and Hitler are now forty-five years in the past,
our memory still is haunted by both—and the 55 million dead of
the war. No event in human history has been "larger" than World
War II; no evil has been greater than that inflicted by Nazi Germany on itself and on the rest of the world. Was not Germany's
unification in 1871 the root of it all? And are we not about to
witness the remake today? Certainly by reasoning backward, we
are quick to discover a tidy chain of historical necessity which
leads from German unification to global disaster.

The story begins on January 18, 1871, when the modern German empire was proclaimed at Versailles. On that fateful day,
Prussia doubled its victory over France by conquering Germany,
as it were. Willing or not, a bunch of ancient kingdoms, prin-
cipalities, duchies, and cities was swept into the Second Reich by
Bismarck's Prussia. Its very name spelled an ominous challenge to
the European order. The First Reich had been the Holy Roman
Empire of the German Nation (962–1806), which saw itself as
heir to Rome and thus to much of Europe. Replacing the old
Reich's pretensions with real strength, the Wilhelminian Empire
quickly turned into the powerhouse of Europe. Dynamic and
restless, ebullient but unsure of itself, the new Reich shouldered
its way to the table of the Great Powers when the chips were
already well-distributed. And so, Germany was bound to threaten
all the established players and, in turn, to be threatened by them.

Bad timing was compounded by the curse of geography.
Plunked down in the middle of Europe, the Reich was stuck with
a highly vulnerable position. Saddled with long, "unnatural"
frontiers and surrounded by heavyweight rivals, the new Germany easily fell for a twin temptation. At home, democracy (moving forward fitfully in Britain and France) was sacrificed to the
imperatives of national power, and nationalism, the heady cry of
"us against them," was proffered as a substitute for liberty and
equality. The second temptation, fed by an accelerating cycle of
paranoia and aggressiveness, was in the cult of the strategic offensive. If each and all were begrudging Germany its "place in the
sun," if the Reich was beset by France in the West, by Russia in the
East, and by Britain from across the sea, why not break the stran-
glehold once and for all? World War I was triggered by a terrorist
murder in Sarajevo, but in truth it represented Germany's ruth-
less attempt to solve its endemic security problem by reaching for
all-out hegemony.

Failure led to defeat, revolution, and the doomed democratic experiment of the Weimar Republic—and a mere twenty years later to the vastly more brutal and bloody second try. The aftermath of the Third Reich is still with us. German and East European Jewry was annihilated. Europe's frontiers were redrawn. Soviet armies encamped in the heart of Europe, and they are beginning to withdraw only now, almost half a century after marching all the way to the Elbe River. Eastern Europe has regained its freedom, but it will take decades to clear away the rubble left behind by Nazi and then Soviet imperialism. Western Europe recovered long ago, but who could have predicted such a happy outcome while surveying the moribund continent on V-E Day?

And now, on the threshold of "Germany, united fatherland," it is feared that the vicious cycle of unification and catastrophe will begin anew. Cartoonists and columnists in America, France, and Britain have been inordinately fond of the image of the Fourth Reich, thus dragging the past 120 years of German history forward into the future. To be sure, the analogy is seductive not only to the pundits and pencil wielders. For all of us feel—indeed, *know*—that an era is coming to an end.

The era just ending, though flawed by ideological and physical partition, has given us the comfort of almost immutable stability. A resurgent West Germany was safely harnessed to the West, and the power of Germany as a whole was nicely neutralized in two countervailing alliances. For some forty years, postwar Germany dared not—and could not—use its economic muscle and geographic advantage in the kind of contest that had brought grief to Europe and the world during the Second Thirty Years' War. But now the European game is changing, and a soon-to-be reunited Germany again will be the number-one player. Will "a new wave of darkness" spread forth from Germany once more?

Tempting as the historical analogies may be, they are almost completely wrong. Anybody reasoning forward from past disaster will be hard put to make the indictment stick. Search and dig as he may, he will scarcely find the social, political, or economic ingredients in contemporary Germany that poisoned the Wilhelminian Empire and the Weimar Republic. For starters, just look at the vignettes of the very recent past—since the Berlin Wall was breached on November 9 of last year.

Though American anchormen, descending in droves on Germany on that occasion, breathlessly announced that Bonn's parliamentarians had risen to intone *Deutschland über alles,* they got their lyrics wrong. In fact, the Bundestag deputies were singing *Einigkeit und Recht und Freiheit* ("Unity, Justice, Freedom"), and not the tainted words of the pre-1945 national anthem which the world has come to see as the very epitome of German national hubris. Even more telling was the song of the young people dancing atop the Berlin Wall that night: *So ein Tag, so wunderschön wie heute* ("What a Day, What a Beautiful Day"). That is the traditional ditty of German soccer fans celebrating the victory of their team; played at a leisurely three-quarter beat, the tune does not quite make it as a rabble-rouser. Amid popping champagne corks, the emotions were those of a family reunion—not the bloody-minded reflexes of unshackled nationalism. People got drunk on booze, not on *Volk* and *Vaterland.*

In West Germany, nobody was thronging through the streets of Frankfurt, Munich, or Hamburg to clamor for *Anschluss.* Indeed, *nobody* was marching—except those East Germans who streamed through the Wall with the incredulous wonderment that might befall inmates suddenly left in charge of the jailhouse. Not *Deutschland* raised their heartbeats, but kiwis and bananas, those symbols of untasted luxury which they carted home by the bushel. In March, during the first free election in East Germany in fifty-seven years, almost half the electorate cast their ballots for the conservative Alliance for Germany, surrogates of Helmut Kohl's Christian Democrats (CDU). And they shunted aside the Social Democrats (SPD) for a simple, powerful reason.

While the SPD wanted to go slow, the Chancellor and his cohorts in Bonn stood for quick monetary and economic union. And in the minds of East Germans, that message read not *Deutschland über alles* but *Deutschemark über alles.* Kohl was the "White Knight" from across the Elbe, extending a friendly takeover offer that would turn sinking Prusso-socialism into a subsidiary of fabulously rich Bonn, Inc. East-marks, fetching at one point only ten West German pfennigs on the black market, would be converted one-for-one into the real thing. To the Saxons and Thuringians, unity evoked not the glory of a reconstituted fatherland but above all the shortest of shortcuts to West German capitalism.

There may be a larger point in this that transcends the two

Germanys: nationalism isn't what it used to be—not in the democratic-industrial segment of the world that stretches from Berkeley to Berlin. Compare 1990 to 1890. How easy it was then to mobilize entire nations around shibboleths like "the white man's burden," "Remember the *Maine*," and "*Gott strafe England*" ("May God Punish England"). Millions went to their deaths in 1914 because their *patrie*, *Vaterland*, or *rodina* so demanded. From 1789 to 1945, European history was written by nations in arms, and nationalism was the murderous energy that drove and sustained them.

Today one has to travel farther afield to observe that blood-fueled engine in action—to Africa and Asia. Thirty thousand Frenchmen were enough to conquer Algeria in 1830, twenty times as many could not hold it in 1962. Six million tons of explosives were dropped on Vietnam, three times more than on Nazi Germany, yet Ho Chi Minh's armies prevailed over the United States. Not Westerners but Arabs, be it in Lebanon or against Israel, today act out their tribal fantasies and obsessions with collective mayhem. Human-wave attacks, *de rigueur* for Frenchmen and Germans in the trenches of Flanders, have now become a specialty of Iranians—who thought very little of using their own children as living mine-sweepers.

Conquest and carnage in the name of nation or faith, then, are no longer a Western pastime; they have been extruded to the Third World, including the southern reaches of the Soviet empire. Perhaps nationalist frenzy will stage a comeback where nationality has been suppressed for so long—in Eastern Europe, the Balkans, and Russia. But in the Euro-Atlantic world, which will soon encompass all of Germany, World War II may have been the last gasp of the "violent and poetical excitement to arms," as Tocqueville called it. What we witness today between Nottingham and Naples is a pale copy of the real thing.

The nation-state is alive and well, but in the West the paranoia and hatred that used to whip nations into collective hysteria have wilted, exposing a toothless kind of national consciousness. The contemporary mutation makes for colorful celebrations of Bastille Day or the Fourth of July and, quadriennally, of Olympic victories. Occasionally nationalism still unites a society behind a Falklands-type expedition, and a more private version has sent soccer hoodlums on a rampage in stadiums around Europe (though the underlying emotion probably was boredom rather than chauvinism). Yet otherwise, Western nationalism has gone the way of Rosie the Riveter and Captain America.

Why do yesterday's volcanoes appear to be extinct—in Germany as elsewhere? One reason, though disappearing into the mist of history, is the memory of two world wars. Seventy million dead add up to a powerful taboo. A more enduring reason is nuclear weapons. In the brooding shadow of the atom, national hubris not only invokes the price of national suicide, but, more important, the price is known beforehand. The Kaiser's soldiers left Berlin on August 3, 1914 with the jubilant pledge: "We'll be back for Christmas." Today, they understand that they might not have a city to which to return.

Similarly, the Germans did not know on September 1, 1939 what their country would look like on May 8, 1945; today, in a world of nuclear weapons, they and everybody else can foresee the consequences with horrifying precision. The paralyzing effect of nuclear weapons may also explain why peace is not just the possession of the well-settled Western democracies, but a blessing bestowed on *all* nations, democratic or not, as long as they live in the realm of the "balance of terror." Conversely, the Third World can indulge in collective bloodshed because, beyond the nuclear arena, that luxury does not come with an existential price tag attached.

A third answer is rooted in the nature of contemporary Western society, which no longer seems to harbor the historical sources of jingoism. To "busy giddy minds with foreign quarrels" was Henry IV's deathbed advice to his son and successor. With that counsel, Shakespeare captured an essential condition of chauvinism: intractable internal conflict that makes rulers and elites resort to the diversion of flag-waving. The heyday of Western nationalism, *circa* 1840–1940, also happens to span a century of economic revolution and wrenching political adaptation—and there is more than coincidence in this correlation. Throughout the West, the onslaught of secularization, industrialization, and urbanization—in short, "modernity"—wreaked havoc on societies given to traditional authority, ancient loyalties, and sedate change. The price of modernity was conflict: between workers and owners, Protestants and Catholics, city and country, rulers and ruled.

The "hidden hand of the market" drove peasants off the land and cobblers off the bench, robbing them of their roots and sweeping them into the maws of urban alienation. Fortunes were made and lost in cycles of boom and bust which would draw the multitudes into the production process only to cast them out again at the next downturn. Battered by vast anonymous forces, no society in the West enjoyed a surfeit of individual happiness and political harmony. But in Bismarckian Germany, something else happened—or more precisely, did not happen.

In France, Britain, and the United States uprooted peasants and downtrodden proletarians ultimately became *citizens* for whom the miseries of modernity were blunted by the blessings of democracy. As the franchise trickled down, previously excluded groups gained power and a sense of mastery over their own fates; their voices and their votes mattered. Not so in Bismarckian Germany where economic expansion and democracy went off in opposite directions. "Enrich yourselves, but leave the driving to us," was the message of the ancien régime that ruled the Second Reich. The economic revolution did not unleash a political one; as wealth increased by leaps and bounds, power remained concentrated in the hands of the few.

The mighty Reich was a class- and conflict-ridden society, mortgaged to a bourgeoisie that had sold away its birthright to the old aristocracy. Nationalism was the savior of that tottering construction, the cement that held it all together. For nationalism is that wondrous "political good" which is never scarce and which bestows psychic equality on rich and poor, on masters and servants alike. Chauvinism, moreover, came easy to a nation that had only recently joined the ranks of the Great Powers, provoking the other players merely by dint of its existence. In a threatening world, the appeal to discipline, duty, and fatherland did not require much mendacity; it was a message any German could understand.

The Weimar Republic was a replay in a far more noxious setting. The Second Reich, after all, was born in national triumph; the Weimar Republic was the product of national disaster. Bismarck and successors presided over an expanding economy; Weimar Germany was a basket case kept alive by infusions of (mainly) American loans. In the late 19th century, Berlin was the diplomatic master of Europe; Germany after World War I was a political outcast, forever humbled by the victors who had imposed a punitive peace in Versailles. There was democracy, to be sure, but the experiment was tainted from the very beginning by the shame of defeat and the toll of economic failure. Perhaps the

Germans still might have made it, in spite of the hyperinflation of 1923 that turned society upside-down. But then the Depression hit. It sharpened ancient class conflicts while disaster after disaster, denying any respite, left only room for delusion and paranoia.

Into that void of rationality and faith stepped, as if made to order by a Satanic god, the pseudo-messianic figure of Hitler. The Fuehrer promised deliverance, rebirth, and salvation—with a message that more and more Germans were only too willing to swallow. Democracy? That was the alien faith of the victors. Freedom? That was but the privilege of the "plutocrats" and the "parasites" who, in cahoots with the "politicians," were sucking the lifeblood out of the honest working man. For people in the grip of economic agony, submission to *Volk* and Fuehrer spelled instant, reassuring equality which the cruel hand of the market would never yield. And Hitler offered them more than just equality. Whether rich or poor, high-born or humble, any German was now a member of the master-race destined to vanquish the enemy within (the Jews) and the enemy without (Russian Bolsheviks and Western capitalists) who, together, had conspired to enslave the German nation.

The moral of this tale is a simple one. By no stretch of the imagination is the Federal Republic, though to be fused soon with its East German brother, a precursor of the Fourth Reich. How do we know? Germans today are inordinately fond of telling themselves and others: "We have learned our historical lesson," meaning: "We were bad then, but we are good now, and therefore you should trust us."

Such incantations, though earnestly uttered, are beside the point. We do not bestow a clean bill of health on an ex-junkie just on his say-so. We look for more tangible proof: does he hold down a job, does he avoid bad company, do his life circumstances keep him from temptation? The real point is that, *objectively,* contemporary West Germany bears little resemblance to the Bismarckian Empire or the Weimar Republic; nor does the Federal Republic live in the same world that its predecessors occupied. In its essential features, it is like any advanced Western society, moving no longer along the *Sonderweg,* the path of separate development, that set previous incarnations of Germany apart from Britain, France, and the United States.

To begin with, democracy works in West Germany, whereas it

was absent in the Second Reich (1871–1991) and doomed in the First Republic (1919–33). And it works not because the new German is "good," while his grandparents were "bad," but because the objective conditions are, for once, benign. Like its Weimar precursor, the Federal Republic was born in defeat, dismemberment, and humiliation. Yet this time two debilitating ingredients were mercifully absent: economic catastrophe and a real sense of renewed war.

The difference between 1919 and 1945 was the cold war, which soon turned a pariah into an indispensable ally. Instead of reparations, there was Marshall Plan aid. Instead of competitive devaluations and beggar-thy-neighbor tariffs, there was free trade and monetary expansion in the context of GATT, the World Bank, and the IMF, institutions built and managed by the United States. Trade outlets lost in the East were doubled and tripled by the Common Market in the West, fueling steady, export-led growth. Paradoxically, even dismemberment and partition proved a boon, feeding, until the Wall was built in 1961, twelve million refugees into a booming economy where labor was soon becoming a scarce commodity.

Unlike the Weimar Republic, the Bonn Republic could *enjoy* the economic consequences of peace; and, as a result, democracy flourished. But just as important, the politics were also right. The great loser of World War I, Weimar Germany, could never clear the accounts. It remained the object of suspicion and the victim of foreign imposition. Not so the Federal Republic. Soon the outcast was handed membership in a Western community that delivered shelter and a role. Instead of French intervention, there was Franco-German friendship. Instead of endemic insecurity, there was NATO and a junior partnership with the United States. For once, Germany was not alone but firmly embedded in the West. And because West German—and European—security was guaranteed by a mighty superpower, the Federal Republic was blessed twice: it could not threaten others—and it could not be threatened by them. To exaggerate a bit, West German democracy was the sturdy child of the cold war and an American-sponsored Western community.

Safety and prosperity prepared the grounds where the seeds of civility, democracy, and, yes, "Westernization" could take root after 1945—as they could not after 1919. In the beginning, there were just the letters of a constitution patterned largely after the American model. But as time went on, a political miracle unfolded that was even more impressive than its vaunted economic twin. Maybe Germans are very *gründlich* (thoroughly efficient) at anything they do, be it totalitarianism or democracy. But the fact is that they excelled in the democratic game in ways none dared predict on the day the Nazi nightmare was crushed by American and Russian tanks.

As time went on, Western democracy—rejected after 1871 and 1919 and torn to shreds after 1933—came to rest on a stronger foundation than just obeisance to the loaded guns of the victors. Here are some of the way-stations. In the 1950's, the extremist parties of the Right and the Left, new Nazis and old Communists, fell into oblivion one by one. [Footnote: Two parties were expressly outlawed. Founded in 1949, the Socialist Reich party (SRP), a Nazi surrogate, was declared illegal by the Constitutional Court in 1952. The Communists (KPD) suffered the same fate in 1956.] Even the party of the Eastern refugees (BHE), beholden to revisionist and nationalist rhetoric, withered away as its members found a place and prosperity in the newly rich Federal Republic. [Footnote: The fate of the Eastern refugees makes for an instructive contrast with the Arab refugees from the wars against Israel. The Germans from Silesia, Pomerania, Bohemia, etc. were rigorously integrated into the Federal Republic so as to blunt the edge of revisionism. In order to keep revanchism alive, the Palestinian refugees were deliberately interned in camps around Israel by Arab regimes.]

In the early 1960's, the democratic constitutional mechanism passed its first critical test in a battle between the freedom of the press and the powers of the executive. Following the orders of Defense Minister Franz-Josef Strauss, the police occupied the building of the *Spiegel* magazine, arresting key editors on the charge of treason in connection with a story on the armed forces. Strauss was later exonerated by the courts, but in the meantime, he had been forced to resign for reasons that recall Richard Nixon's fall: trying to cover up his role in the affair, he had lied to parliament. For a society that had only recently come to live by the rule of law and the separation of powers, that outcome augured well for the future.

About once every decade after the war, civilian supremacy was tested by individual members of the military establishment (though never as brutally as in the encounter during the Korean War between General Douglas MacArthur and President Harry Truman). In each case, the civilian authorities prevailed—and the generals resigned. The 1970's witnessed the rise of terrorism, complete with spectacular murders of business leaders. Predictably, there was a cry for harsher laws and greater police powers. In the end, though, civil rights were not curtailed, apart from the ugly *Extremistenbeschluss* that barred radicals from the civil service—be they lowly railroad workers or high defense officials. The Constitutional Court, at first the weakest of the three branches, successively took a page out of *Marbury* v. *Madison,* asserting its powers against the executive and establishing its right not just to interpret but to make the law according to constitutional principle. This is a far cry from Weimar, where the judiciary would often serve rather than check the powers that be.

More and more, Bonn turned out to be anything but Weimar. Yet in the 1960's, memories of the 1930's suddenly returned with a vengeance. In mid-decade, the Federal Republic experienced its first serious recession. Half-a-million people were out of work, and that correlated ominously with the rise of the neo-Nazi National Democratic party (NPD). So Bonn was like Weimar after all? The specter, however, soon dissipated, and today, the NPD garners less than 1 percent at the polls. If Bonn *were* Weimar, it should be getting a great deal more. Throughout much of the 1980's, unemployment has hovered around two million (about 8 percent of the workforce), yet the neo-Nazis are on the verge of extinction.

What then of the cynically mislabeled Republikaners, a bunch of populists, nationalists, and xenophobes who started making headlines last year? They gained their first parliamentary seats in the West Berlin regional assembly in January 1989, and they soared to worrisome prominence in the elections to the European parliament five months later (7.2 percent nationwide). Yet today they languish below 3 percent in the opinion polls, and in the most recent state elections, in high-unemployment Saarland, a rustbelt region, they fetched only 3.3 percent.

The reason may be an old one in the annals of electoral politics. A protest vote does not a party make, and sheer resentment, in which the Republikaners try to trade, does not make for stable voting allegiances—at least not in a basically well-settled society. Unlike Weimar Germany, the Federal Republic is not afflicted with personal misery and collective humiliation—at worst only with sheer boredom. After a while, the novelty of an "anti-party" party wears off, and the flock returns to the established organizations which, by then, have stolen the anti-party's thunder by promising cheap housing and job programs. Unemployment, even of the permanent kind, does not thrust its victims into the lumpenproletariat—thanks to a lavish welfare net extended by the government.

The larger point is that the modern Western welfare state—in Germany as elsewhere—has plenty of defenses against the revolt of the losers. In the 1920's, an impoverished young German might have joined the Storm Troopers for the sake of a fresh brown shirt, three meals a day, and the social status conferred by a shiny pair of jackboots. Today, his out-of-work grandchild gets two-thirds of his last after-tax income from the unemployment office, and he does not even have to pick it up; it is deposited in his bank account. More important, he does not have to attend a mass rally in order to relieve his boredom. Instead he can pop a video into his machine, or spend his welfare check in sunny, cheap Mallorca. In short, the nature of contemporary Western society is such that even the disadvantaged can satisfy their personal needs in personal ways; they need not submit to a Fuehrer or collective. And that cuts down the business opportunities of Pied Pipers.

Those who fear a "new wave of darkness" simply overlook how much Germany today is part of the Western mainstream. The Republikaners resemble Jean-Marie Le Pen's National Front in France more than they do the SA or NSDAP of yore. They resent high housing prices, cultural permissiveness, the high-tech plant next door that offers no employment to the unskilled, and the influx of foreigners, even those "foreigners" who are East Germans or German ethnics coming in from Russia, Romania, or Poland. Adding the extremes of the Right and Left in Germany today, one arrives at an electoral potential of 10, or at the outside 15, percent, most of which is enveloped by the traditional parties. But that is no different from France, Britain, or Italy.

Anti-Semitism? *Measured* anti-Semitism is less in the Federal Republic than in some other Western countries. [Footnote: In a four-country survey, fewer Germans expressed negative stereotypes about Jews than Austrians, Frenchmen, and Americans. Generally, anti-Semitism is higher in Austria than in West Germany. In 1952, 37 percent of a West German sample agreed to the proposition, "It is better for Germany to have no Jews in the country." In 1983, that proportion had declined to 9 percent. For an exhaustive survey of public attitudes, see Renate Köcher,

Deutsche und Juden vier Jahrzehnte danach (Allensbach: Institut für Demoskopie). Data were collected in 1986.] But these figures must be taken with a grain of salt. First, anti-Semitism in Germany is still imbued with a powerful taboo—so powerful that respondents will undoubtedly conceal it from the professional pulse-takers. Second, there are scarcely any Jews left to hate in Germany. The Jewish community encompasses about 30,000 registered members, and there may be another 10,000 who do not proclaim their religious affiliation. That is a far cry from the 600,000 German Jews before the war. A more profound reason for the lack of visible anti-Semitism is the invisibility of the targets. Jews in West Germany do not occupy the prominent positions their expelled or slaughtered co-religionists held in the prewar period: as bankers, journalists, scientists, and academics.

Nonetheless, the obvious ought not be ignored. Anti-Semitism in the Federal Republic remains a cultural and political no-no, and when it raises its ugly head, it is swiftly slapped down, be it by the authorities or by published opinion.

East Germany, however, was quite different. There, the Communist regime started out in the late 1940's by simply absolving the "Worker and Peasant State" from all crimes; these, after all, had been committed by the "bad" Germans in the reactionary West. Thereafter, the regime faithfully followed every twist and turn of the anti-Semitic line laid down by Moscow—from Stalin's purges to the bureaucratic repression under Brezhnev, when anti-Semitism took on the convenient but no less vicious guise of anti-Zionism. Today, there are only a few hundred Jews in the GDR.

Yet this ugly tale comes with a semi-happy ending. On April 13, the GDR's parliament asked "the Jews in all the world for forgiveness"—for the "hypocrisy and hostility of official GDR policy against the state of Israel and for the persecution and degradation of Jews in our country even after 1945." Confessing "shame and grief," the East German parliament accepted responsibility for Nazi crimes and pledged material restitution—something the Communist regime had never done.

On the verge of reunification, Germany does not look like that "strange and eerie place" so many worried observers descry as the precursor of the Fourth Reich. Indeed, in some respects, the Federal Republic is a more liberal polity than either France or Britain. Power is more diffused in the West German federal system (which will also be extended to the East) than in centralized France, and there is no Official Secrets Act that so hamstrings the press in Britain. (Keeping a state secret in Bonn is harder even than in Washington.) Compared with Helmut Kohl, Mrs. Thatcher enjoys almost dictatorial powers, and compared with the "republican monarchy" that is France, the Federal Republic is a political free-for-all. West German democracy, as the past forty years suggest, is not a fly-by-night operation that will vanish at the next economic downturn.

The problem lies elsewhere, and it stems not from the internal workings of the Federal Republic but from the external setting of a reunited Germany. The reassuring career of the Bonn Republic cannot be divorced from the ultra-stable European order installed after 1945—and which is going fast. The postwar order was built in and around Germany, and it had two functions. Explicitly, it was to contain the might of Soviet Russia; implicitly, it was to envelop the energies of a resurgent Germany. In historical terms, the postwar order was "just right": it protected Germany against others and against itself; it pulled the sting of Russian as well as of German power; and it achieved all this not by imposition and discrimination, but by community and integration. Paranoid nationalism cannot fester when safety is assured within so cozy a framework. Yet with Russia receding and containing itself, as it were, the whole structure is losing its *raison d'être* and claim to allegiance.

With Russian retracting, Germany will become number one on the continent—willy-nilly and by sheer dint of economic clout and geographic position. Yet at this point, there is nothing to replace the *ancien système* that functioned so ingeniously to keep the dynamic part of Germany both happy and harnessed. To be sure, NATO and the European Community (EC) are still alive, while their Eastern counterparts, the Warsaw Pact and Comecon, are moving into the dustbin of history. On the other hand, if Russia turns inward for any length of time, NATO will not flourish and the EC will not become what its founding fathers envisioned: a West European common market blossoming into political union.

Take NATO. Add a united Germany [Footnote: The current scheme, favored by Bonn as well as its allies, is to incorporate all of Germany into NATO, but keep NATO troops out of East German territory. Accordingly, the GDR enters into NATO, but NATO does not enter into the GDR.], factor in a democratic

Eastern Europe, and subtract the Soviet threat. What do you get? Something called NATO, but which, successively, will be emptied of its reality. An alliance of democracies, it cannot resist what is gnawing at its sinews already—"competitive disarmament" in search of a "peace dividend." Ground-launched nuclear weapons—short-range missiles and nuclear artillery—will be the first to go. And in all fairness, it is hard to come up with a rationale for such weapons once their intended targets (Russian armies) are gone, leaving in place Czechs, Poles, and Hungarians who have neither the will nor the wherewithal to make a decent enemy. Nuclear weapons in a forward position, however, are not add-on frills but the very embodiment of America's security guarantee to Western Europe—and a brake on the acquisition of national deterrents.

For the core of the alliance is not so much the Washington Treaty of 1949 as NATO's flesh-and-steel arrangements on West German soil. The Federal Republic is home to 250,000 American troops, to 55,000 British and 50,000 French soldiers, and to Belgian, Dutch, and Canadian units. Except for the French, these and almost half-a-million West German troops are all integrated in a multinational command structure that is the essence of NATO. With the Russians withdrawing and the Warsaw Pact withering away, what would these forces do? Whom would they contain, especially once they had been whittled down to token contingents? Would they stand watch on the Elbe River—beyond which there is nothing left to guard? The point of these questions is to cast the cold light of realism on notions according to which NATO will persist while the Soviet Union and the Warsaw Pact disappear from the equation. An alliance is logically inseparable from the idea of a threat and a foe, and if the latter wanes, so will the former.

Today it is anybody's guess how many American troops will remain in Germany—and who else would take them once the Congress and/or the Germans decided they were no longer needed. The burden of a Great-Power role has never sat well on American shoulders; historically, at least, the task was only assumed when a nasty hegemonist lurked across the water: Kaiser Bill, Adolf Hitler, Hirohito, Joseph Stalin. Gorbachev, for the time being, does not quite fit that profile, and so George McGovern's 1972 campaign cry of "Come home, America" might finally come true. Yet few people realize how crucial America's role in Europe has been—not just as protector but also as pacifier, as the player who not only held off Stalin but also took the edge off the ancient rivalries that had embroiled Britain, France, and Germany in periodic war. With the United States ensconced in the system, there was suddenly a power greater than all of them that could ensure each against the perils of cooperation.

In that respect, NATO-builders Truman and Eisenhower were also the real founding fathers of the European Community. Yet the EC as we know it will not survive the cold war, either. Suitably reformed, Hungary, Poland, Czechoslovakia, and Romania have at least as much of a claim to entry as had Portugal and Greece. Why keep out Switzerland, Sweden, and Austria once the EC is no longer the economic core of a Western defense organization? One thing is certain. More members equal more heterogeneity which, in turn, will postpone political union *sine die*. With NATO reduced to a symbolic compact, and the EC to a European-wide free-trade zone, what will lend strength and resilience to a post-postwar Europe dominated by Germany?

While proclaiming fealty to NATO, German leaders in Bonn, Berlin, and Dresden already are speculating about "transcending the alliances." The vision is of an "all-European peace order" that would produce "collective security" in the framework of the 35-nation Conference on Security and Cooperation in Europe (CSCE). [Footnote: The CSCE encompasses all the European nations plus the United States, Canada, and the Soviet Union. It lacks a secretariat and a structure, and it requires unanimity for all decisions. Since 1975, the CSCE has done some useful work on the periphery of classic security policy, e.g., by sponsoring "confidence-building measures" such as limits on military maneuvers and their timely announcement.] That approach—effective sanctions by the peace-lovers against the aggressor—was last tried by the League of Nations when fascist Italy grabbed Abyssinia. (Haile Selassie went into exile, and the League went on to its unheralded demise.) "Collective security" is to alliance what a Dodge City posse is to the FBI—a somewhat haphazard attempt to make nations follow duty rather than self-interest. Collective security is also the daily fare of the United Nations as it is asked to bring the world's weight to bear on Arabs and Israelis, Iraqis and Iranians, Khmer Rouge and rival Cambodians. It does not work today, as it did not work then, because nations are loath to sacrifice their *sacro egoismo* on the altar of abstract justice. Lofty as it is, the precept of "one for all, and all for one" has a fatal flaw: it requires nations to behave so virtuously as to render the mechanism of "collective security" unnecessary. The system *assumes* stability; it cannot create it.

If the old structures go, an "all-European peace order"—
a.k.a. "collective security," where each is tied to all and thus to
none—hardly will be able to assume the functions of the old
regime. Which leads to the major question. If, as I have argued,
the happy career of the Federal Republic was part and parcel of a
sturdy postwar order, what will transpire inside the country once
a mighty Germany bestrides a European stage that is no longer
dominated by the old props and players?

The bet is (even odds, no more) that Germany will *not* become
a "strange and eerie place." Once the horrendous costs of re-
habilitating the East have been absorbed, the heirs to Wilhelm II,
Weimar, and the Wehrmacht probably will use their clout less
hesitantly than in the past. Nor will the Germans defer so frequently to allies and neighbors as a reduced demand for security
cuts into their need for allegiance and as the burden of guilt
feelings is lightened with each passing generation. But a replay of
Wilhelm II or Adolf H.? Interstate rivalry in Europe—indeed, in
the entire democratic-industrial world—has evolved onto more
mercantile levels as the currency of military force has become
devalued. Pearl Harbor is no longer bombed, but bought, by the
Japanese. The Germans no longer invade the Alsace; they *pay* for
choice plots there. And the Alsatian farmers would rather sell out
to the *boches* than eke out a miserly living on lands rendered
unprofitable by the EC bureaucracy in Brussels.

While the demise of the postwar order will liberate German
power above all, a nation's power today is not measured by possession, but by the answer to questions such as: "Who determines
parities in the European currency grid?" It so happens that it is
the German Bundesbank, which grates hard on French monetary
authorities, and understandably so. But this is still a different
contest than was played out with German jackboots on the pavements of Paris fifty years ago. The battle lines are drawn in the
balance-of-payments ledgers, and the accounts are settled with
ECU's (the EC internal currency), not with blood and iron. The
rivalry is acted out in an arena where joint welfare, not this or that
province, is the stake—where your losses are not my gains, but
where we both win and lose together. The victims of Sony may
resent cheap VCR's made in Japan, but who would go to war over
the privilege of buying worse-quality goods at higher prices?
Americans may brandish military metaphors when it comes to
Japan, but in truth they think about improving the educational
and management system at home, not about sending the Marines
into MITI.

The game of nations in the democratic-industrial world has changed, as have these nations themselves—including Germany. *"Nach Paris!"* today is not the battle cry of a Wehrmacht lieutenant departing Berlin Central in search of booty and glory, but the civilized request of an amorous German student buying a round-trip ticket in order to visit his French girlfriend. In such societies, given to the *individual* pursuit of happiness, the Pied Pipers of nationalism will not attract many followers.

But might not Germany unshackled hanker after nuclear weapons and push for the revision of its Eastern frontiers? That is impossible to exclude, but hard to imagine. The new, more civilized and civilianized game of nations offers the largest payoffs to nations such as Germany and Japan. The game has devalued the military chips, delivering power and prestige to those who can back up their bets with investments and loans. Why then should they forgo their advantage by changing the rules? In the attempt, they would certainly revive the hostile coalitions that proved their undoing in 1945. And one must assume that well-settled democracies are more sensible and sensitive about such risks than were the Hohenzollerns and the Hitlerites.

Soon Germany will be reunited. But the remake will not be shot with a cast of latter-day Erich von Stroheims. The sound track will not be the *Horst-Wessel-Lied,* the fighting song of the Nazis, but a reggae or rhythm-and-blues tune. Cologne and Kansas City, Munich and Marseilles, have been listening to the same beat for a long time; adding Dresden and Leipzig should not ruin that score. At least, we are entitled to hope so.

ÜBER THE HILL[3]

Helmut Kohl is a bit plump for the part of Siegfried, Wagner's idealized all-German hero. Yet it is as a kind of modern Siegfried that Kohl has been portrayed in the American media since his triumph as the chancellor of German unity last year. A tide of

[3]Article by Niall Ferguson, Cambridge fellow and lecturer in modern European history, from *The New Republic* 204:24,26–7 F 4 '91. Copyright © 1991 by *The New Republic.* Reprinted by permission.

popular enthusiasm for reunification ensured his victory in December's elections, we are told. And now the Rhinegold of an even larger German economy will confer measureless might on the man from the Palatinate—and on his expanded country. Despite Germany's apparent irrelevance in the Gulf crisis, the united country, according to Timothy Garton Ash in *The New York Review of Books*, is set to be "once again the great power at the center of Europe."

Will it? Such views of German reunification rest on two questionable assumptions: first, that a united Germany will be a more nationalist Germany, imbued with a new sense of self-confidence and national pride; and second, that a bigger Germany must be a stronger Germany—that territorial expansion will inevitably lead to economic growth, and thus to greater German international power.

In all of this, a skewed reading of German history has played a critical role. According to this view, the first united Germany rose to world power, thanks to dynamic economic growth, only to end in the horrors of the Third Reich, thanks to an excess of nationalist sentiment. But this is a distortion. In fact, if history is any guide to the future, it suggests that the new Germany will be far from nationalist, and economically weaker than its West German predecessor—a far cry from the assertive superpower of popular imagination.

Consider first the idea that Germany will now have more national self-confidence. In fact, none of the factors that historians believe led to the rise of radical nationalism in post-1870 Germany exists any longer. The cultural tradition of nation-worship, pumped into Germans by generations of shrill professors, is all but extinct. And reactionary social groups like the old Prussian aristocracy, big business, and the petite bourgeoisie have declined, or changed their political ways.

If anything, the intellectual elites treat any hint of Reich-envy with the kind of withering contempt most American professors direct to exhibitions of political incorrectness. In the West educators have striven to create a "postnational" society; in the East, an "anti-fascist" one. To be sure, there are still some social groups attracted by nationalist tub-thumping, but they are marginal, not the phalanx of middle-class voters who supported radical nationalism between 1890 and 1933. Today's neo-Nazis, the Republicans (no relation), are provincial malcontents and hooligans whose main plank is anti-immigration. They did well at elections in Berlin and Baden-Württemberg in 1989. But as with previous West German neo-Nazi bubbles, the Reps' soon burst. As an anti-immigration nationalist party, they foundered when a wave of immigration brought about national reunification.

What about the East Germans? There is some evidence that old-style nationalism has proved more resilient under "real existing socialism" than under liberal democracy, and that unemployed East Germans may vent their frustrations on immigrants from farther east. But there is equally persuasive evidence of the persistence of socialist sentiment in the East, in spite of the last forty years. Neither sentiment has manifested itself in East German voting patterns. The truth is the East Germans have voted consistently for the Kohl coalition: for the conservative CDU and the liberal Free Democrats.

Nationalism is less likely as a social consequence of reunification than a revival of regionalism and secularism. Five newly reconstituted states, each with a strong historical identity, are already making competing claims for help in reconstruction, reviving old East-West rivalries and adding to the more familiar cash-battles between North and South. Reunification also shifts the Federal Republic's center of gravity away from Kohl's Catholic Rhineland and closer to Foreign Minister Hans-Dietrich Genscher's Protestant Saxony-Anhalt. After forty years of a Catholic majority in the Federal Republic, the confessional balance is once again Protestant. That may well dilute the South German Catholic values that have proved so enduring in the Federal Republic, and boost the more secular attitudes on divorce and abortion that have been the Protestant legacy elsewhere in Europe.

The new Germany is unlikely, then, to be particularly nationalist. But will it be economically strong? Even optimists admit that the short-term answer is no. The sheer cost of reunification will weigh down the German economy for some time to come. Since the leap in the dark of monetary and economic unification on July 1, 1990, the government has been spending money hand over fist to avoid a collapse in the East and a mass exodus. At the same time, to reassure West German taxpayers, Kohl plagiarized a pre-election pledge: "No new taxes." Even now, with Finance Minister Theo Waigel unveiling a package of budget cuts, privatizations, and levies, reunification is still largely being financed on credit. The public sector deficit for 1990 will be around 100 billion deutsche marks. This year's is estimated at 140 billion DM, over 5 percent of projected national income. By the end of 1991 the total public debt could reach 1.3 trillion DM—perhaps as much as 54 percent of national income, up from 20 percent in 1970.

It is a situation that Americans will recognize. What may not so readily strike them is that a parallel also lies in the German past. In September 1870 Otto von Bismarck—the German chancellor from 1871 to 1890, to whom Kohl is often improbably compared—made a revealing remark to his son after negotiations with the defeated French. "I said," wrote Bismarck, "that we will talk about the money later; first we want to determine the German frontier." Unity first and hang the cost. True, the defeated French contributed; but within a few years, as the costs of running the new nation continued to rise, Bismarck's Reich had begun to borrow. By 1891 total public debt as a fraction of national income had increased to over 50 percent compared with a figure of 15 percent for Prussia at the start of the wars of unification. It rose steadily (peaking at 120 percent) until the monarchy's demise, as defense spending rocketed before and during the First World War.

This process was repeated by the next two German regimes: the Weimar Republic and the Third Reich. Between 1924 and 1945 the public debt, in proportion to national income, soared fifty-fold. Moreover, each phase of state-building triggered inflation. Unification in 1870 was followed by a brief inflationary boom and bust on the back of French reparations; the early 1900s built up inflationary pressures that boiled over after 1914, leading to the hyperinflation of 1923. There was a similar inflationary cycle from about 1936 to 1947.

Could it happen again? Certainly a third hyperinflation is not in the cards: the vital monetary constraints, now imposed by the independent Bundesbank, have not been removed as they were in 1914 and 1933, and inflation is expected to remain just below the OECD average of 3 to 4 percent in the coming two years. Nevertheless, the economic burden of this rising debt should not be underestimated, particularly when so much of the money is being spent on non-productive job creation, and when the world economic outlook is so shaky.

There's nothing, after all, historically inevitable about German economic expansion. Growth in the last united Germany tended to be specific to certain regions—the Rhineland, for example—

rather than to the nation as a whole, which was slowed down by large, backward areas in the rural East and South. Aggregate growth rates were erratic, with "good" phases (1871–74, 1892–1900, 1903–13, and 1934–38) outnumbered by long periods of stagnation (1875–91, 1914–33). The high levels of private investment and productivity growth of the 1890s and 1900s have to be set against the miserable record of Weimar and the Third Reich. And only twice in the whole period of German unity from 1871 to 1945 did the Reich achieve the trade surpluses that have been such a lasting feature of West German success—in the recessions of 1926 and 1931, as imports slumped.

This is not to say that a united Germany inevitably means economic weakness; merely that it doesn't necessarily mean economic success. If anything, the worry is not whether five East German states will make the German economy stronger, but whether they will make it weaker. With Saxony and Mecklenburg, the West has been burdened with a rustbelt and a rural backwater that will reduce overall growth just as the old East of Prussia used to. Meanwhile, the German trade surplus is set to fall from 49.3 billion DM in 1990 to 17.9 billion DM in 1992, with some analysts predicting that within five years it will have vanished. And for the export-oriented, oil-dependent German economy, war in the Gulf and world recession spell trouble.

The international implications of economic and political unity become clearer if one asks just how far the last united Germany succeeded in turning its economic base into power abroad. In fact, success was limited. Unification itself between 1866 and 1871 was only possible because of an odd combination of Russian and French weakness. The bids by Bismarck's successors, Bernhard von Bülow and Theobald von Bethmann Hollweg, to challenge British naval dominance after 1897 and to check Russian influence in the Ottoman and Austro-Hungarian empires were costly failures. The Reich lacked financial resources to outbuild the British admiralty and establish military hegemony over Central Europe. The final gamble, the First World War, ended in disaster.

This failure to turn economic resources into international clout continued from 1919 to 1931, as successive republican governments sought to avoid paying reparations under the Versailles Treaty. It was only the economic collapse of the West and the moral collapse of the League of Nations that enabled Hitler to embark on his program of expansion and "Aryanization." True, it took the full might of the Anglo-American-Russian alliance to stop him. But the brief, spectacular military success of 1939–41 rested on remarkably shaky economic foundations.

In this light, the current predictions of German world domination seem absurdly overdone, and not just because the new Germany is considerably smaller than the Reich and has a declining population. Again, the parallels between the old and the new Germany are revealing. As in 1870, favorable international circumstances in 1989 and 1990 were more important than domestic leadership in bringing about unity. The economic collapse of the Eastern bloc was the decisive factor, opening the border gate for East German citizens fleeing through Hungary and Czechoslovakia during the summer of 1989. Of equal importance was Western confusion: the Bush administration never hesitated in backing its favorite European ally; but the British and the French failed hopelessly to translate their common reservations into a joint plan for delay.

Such Anglo-French disarray has suggested to many that the new Germany will at least dominate the European Community. But here too there are obstacles. First, the French are edgy, concerned by the upward pressure being exerted on European interest and exchange rates as a result of German unification. Second, Bonn's recent attempt to establish rapport with the new British prime minister, John Major, could founder on the vexed question of EC farm subsidies. Even in Eastern Europe it's hard to see the Germans making much of their position. Unlike their counterparts of a hundred years ago, few German businessmen have faith in *Mitteleuropa* as a market. For most Germans, alarmed at the prospect of mass migration by unemployed Slavs, the region is a source of anxiety rather than a potential sphere of influence. And it seems increasingly likely that the estimated 50 billion DM that Bonn has given to Gorbachev will yield scant reward as reform gives way to reaction.

In other words, a close look at the past suggests the reverse of the conventional wisdom on German reunification. United Germans are not necessarily nationalist Germans. Big Germany is not necessarily mighty Germany. As if to underline the point, the present has also provided a simple test of German superpower status: the Gulf crisis. The test has been flunked. First, the crisis has revealed the full extent of popular anti-militarism. The vast majority of Germans oppose war in the Gulf, despite their economy's heavy dependence on the region's oil. Even the token gesture of sending eighteen Luftwaffe jets to Turkey has caused a public furor. Second, the crisis has revealed the limits of the economy as a source of international power. Several German companies have already broken the U.N. embargo of Iraq, fatally undermining Genscher's preference for relying on sanctions to pry Iraq out of Kuwait. The news that the defense budget is going to be cut to help pay the costs of reunification is a further blow to Germany's world-power status. To imagine Helmut Kohl as Siegfried with a paunch is just about possible. But Siegfried without a sword?

REINVENTING EUROPE[4]

To the postwar generation that grew up with the iron curtain, a glance through the 1936 *Europa Touring Guide* is a shocking reminder of how unnatural the division of Europe has been for the past 40 years. The guidebook, with no hint of the barbed wire and concrete to come, notes that a motorist traveling from Berlin to Krakow crosses only one border. It advises that Albanian customs officers are "very obliging to foreign tourists" and promises that the best French food east of Paris can be found in Warsaw.

Now, the map of Europe that changed so dramatically with World War II is changing again. As the two military alliances that have enforced the division of the Continent begin to give way, new economic arrangements will redraw some boundaries and erase others. Europe's drive toward greater economic unity in the 1990s will revitalize the Old World, but it also could aggravate the strains between Western Europe and the U.S., over trade, over how to assess the Soviet threat and over how deeply to invest in a bankrupt Soviet bloc. Within Western Europe, the ghosts of campaigns past are beginning to reappear, between France and Britain, for example, and now between Germany and its neighbors,

[4]Article by Douglas Stranglin, Clemens P. Work, and Monroe W. Karmin, staff writers, from *U.S. News & World Report.* 107:39–43 N 27, '89. Copyright November 27, 1989 by *U.S. News & World Report.* Reprinted by permission.

about who will lead, who will follow and who should get out of the way. The most volatile region—again—may be Eastern Europe, where the demise of Communism and the retreat of Soviet power already are uncorking old ethnic, religious and national hatreds.

Reform in Eastern Europe comes at a critical time in the Continent's drive toward integration. Some of the toughest issues on the European Community's agenda, such as monetary union, a common West European currency and a social charter guaranteeing workers' basic rights, have yet to be settled. French President François Mitterrand called an emergency EC summit in Paris last weekend to discuss the accelerating changes in Eastern Europe. EC traders, realizing that the huge Western European market now could be expanded to include the hungry consumers of Eastern Europe, want a more ambitious agenda, despite Mikhail Gorbachev's warning to the West last week against "exporting capitalism" into the Kremlin's back yard. Poland, Hungary and now East Germany are wooing Western investors. Czechoslovakia could be next.

New equilibrium. But there could be snags. The changes in Eastern Europe come amid a festering political dispute between Mitterrand and British Prime Minister Margaret Thatcher over deeper economic integration in Western Europe. "We must decide how to manage this new equilibrium," says Corrado Pirzio-Biroli, acting head of the EC delegation to the United States. Because Europe includes so many small countries, the potential size and strength of a united Europe are deceptive. In fact, Greater Europe, which stretches to Poland's eastern border, covers 3.8 million square miles, more than the United States. There are 500 million people in Greater Europe, with nearly 360 million in Western Europe alone. Economically, Western Europe already is a superpower. Its gross domestic product is $5.5 trillion, about 70 percent of the GDP of the U.S. and Japan combined.

To some analysts, it is almost as if history is repeating itself. Richard Bitzinger, a European specialist with the Rand Corporation, notes that the ascendancy of economic power is a throwback to the 17th century, when the Dutch, with their trade routes and colonies, became a major world power despite military weakness. "If power, authority and influence is not measured by military instruments, then what is it measured by?" Bitzinger says. "It used to be that empires were based on trade and economics—and we are moving in that direction again."

But as Europe assumes a larger economic role, it could clash with the United States. In July, President Bush signaled a sea change in Europe's economic role when he conceded to the EC the lead in coordinating aid to Eastern Europe. Last week, West Germany sketched out its design for a "Marshall Plan" for East Germany while Thatcher called on the EC to upgrade its ties with the emerging democracies of Eastern Europe by giving them the association status now enjoyed by Turkey. Bonn's six-point plan for East Germany would include far-reaching investments and joint ventures and even a revamping of the country's communication and transport system. In Washington last week, Solidarity leader Lech Walesa's appeal for "an investment in freedom, democracy and peace" included some gentle chiding of the Bush administration's meager offers when he called for a U.S. commitment "adequate to the greatness of the American nation."

America's go-slow approach derives partly from a belief that the Europeans, particularly the Germans, now have the financial strength to take the lead and partly from a concern that a sudden infusion of big money might be wasted in systems still struggling to cast off Stalinism. In addition, David Wigg, a former U.S. deputy assistant secretary of defense, warns that heavy Western investment in the region could backfire. Unless the Soviet Union has abandoned its traditional expansionist goals, Wigg says, its hands-off posture toward bankrupt Eastern Europe will not be permanent. "I call it a long-term lease with a take-back option," says Wigg. "What they get back is a new and improved building." Wigg and others worry that Western Europe could become so economically embroiled in the East bloc that it will confuse economic and security interests.

There is no doubt that the military alliances will fade in importance; the question is what kinds of structures will take their place. French political scientist Pierre Hassner predicts that NATO and the Warsaw Pact will become "relatively empty shells." "The name of the game is no longer security," he says, "but the mutual influence of societies, what the EC does for Eastern Europe, and what West Germany does for East Germany." Hassner foresees either a Brussels-centered European Common Market, a neutral, Finlandized Europe or a Balkanized Continent, with the prospect of civil war or nationalist clashes in Poland, Yugoslavia or the Soviet Union if economic reforms fail in those countries. "It's a kind of new game," Hassner says, "where Europe increasingly takes on the character of North-South relations. What do you do about immigration, debt? The U.N. may look more relevant than a cornerstone of European military alliances."

Looking both ways. Some Europeans worry that West Germany will lose its enthusiasm for economic unity within the EC. For its part, Bonn feels it can give full attention to both halves of Europe, pledging unfailing loyalty to EC objectives while restoring Eastern Europe's shattered economy. Its economic-aid plan for East Germany would loose West German corporations on the country, encouraging them with tax breaks. That would make West Germany, already the world's fourth-largest economy and biggest exporter, richer than ever. French and U.S. policymakers argue that Bonn's aid plan fits so nicely with East Germany's needs that it could spur reunification, giving rise to a Germany that could drift free of EC restraints to dominate Europe. That fear seems unfounded for now. "Europe is nothing if not Pan-European," observes Paul Gallis, a Western Europe expert with the Congressional Research Service. "West Germany's economic well-being is tied to the EC and the West." Most of West Germany's $75 billion trade surplus is with other European nations. Yet the worry is severe enough that Jacques Delors, president of the European Commission, has pledged that East Germany, once it reformed its stagnant command economy, would be bonded to the EC in some form.

The rich get richer. Despite 28 years of the Berlin Wall, the two Germanys already have extensive ties. Though trade between them is minimal—about $7 billion last year in two-way trade—their relationship is so close that Bonn does not even count shipments to East Germany as exports. Though there are sure to be housing shortages and other bottlenecks, the gradual unification of the two German economies will be a boon to West Germany, already growing at more than 4 percent a year, or double the U.S. rate. A shortage of skilled labor is certain to be alleviated by the influx of refugees from the East. But because these new workers earn so little—about $75 a month in East Germany, or one tenth the average wage in West Germany—they are not expected to push up inflation.

Closer economic ties between the Germanys could increase friction within the EC. "What if West Germany becomes a conduit for low-priced Eastern bloc goods?" asks Philip Hinson, director of Western European affairs with the U.S. Chamber of Commerce. "Other countries will be screaming about dumping." But former EC Vice President Wilhelm Haferkamp counters that other trade safeguards will prevent dumping and that the danger of low-priced goods competing unfairly with Western products will disappear as Eastern economies turn toward capitalism.

How well Bonn manages its delicate balancing act will have enormous implications for the future configuration of global economic power. As Japan has gained on the U.S., Europe has dropped to third-rate status. The goal of Europe 1992 is to promote a renaissance of the Continent crippled by so-called Eurosclerosis that Europe suffered a decade ago. The architects of 1992 hope that by dropping barriers that impede the growth of globally competitive industries, an integrated EC alone can come close to equaling America's $5.2 trillion economy. They could be right. By cooperating on research and development, accelerating the establishment of Pan-European companies and taking other expansionary steps, says William Griffith of the Massachusetts Institute of Technology, Europe could catch up with the U.S. and Japan in five to 10 years.

What happens next in East Germany will affect the way Europe's economic map is redrawn. If East Germany is accorded associate membership in the EC, other countries will surely clamor for the same. Turkey already has requested full admission, and the central debate within the Community will be whether to broaden the EC or deepen the economic commitment of the 12 existing members. Britain's Thatcher is already using the East German upheaval as an excuse to slow progress toward a complete economic union.

Most likely, Europe after 1992 will grow both broader and deeper. Europe could come to resemble a series of concentric circles, EC President Delors theorizes, with the European Commission in the middle and other countries in more-distant rings with less comprehensive ties. In the outer rings, according to this theory, would be members of the European Free Trade Association—Austria, Finland, Iceland, Norway, Sweden and Switzerland. These countries trade freely with the EC without belonging to it.

Two big deals. For the U.S., the changes in Eastern Europe make its stake in the Continent's huge, vibrant market all the more enticing. "We're fools," says lawyer Richard Rivers, a former trade official in the Carter administration, "if we don't get in [to Eastern Europe] and get in there fast." Evidently, the message has begun to be heard. On successive days last week, two large deals were announced, a $100 million glass-making joint venture between Guardian Industries and a Hungarian firm, and General Electric's $150 million purchase of a controlling stake in a Hungarian light-bulb company.

The message also applies to relations with Moscow. Last week, Commerce Secretary Robert Mosbacher and Soviet Foreign Economic Relations Minister Konstantin Katushev announced an agreement to draft a new tax treaty. A decision to begin work on a possible bilateral trade agreement was announced as well, and Katushev, anticipating the possible lowering of U.S. tariffs on Soviet goods, said the U.S.S.R. "will be pleased to see American ladies in Russian furs."

But concerns linger that Europe 1992 could turn into Fortress Europe, a protectionist enclave with higher, not lower, barriers to outsiders. Most observers believe that although the worry has some foundation, mainly due to European fears of Japan's economic might, it is probably overstated, given the EC's already vast economic ties with the U.S.

Though the odds now are heavily in favor of greater EC integration, growing prospects of a global recession could once again stampede frightened nations toward protectionism. Another danger is the fragility of Gorbachev's *perestroika*. "The threat of a Soviet economic collapse could be the Achilles' heel for the EC," says Robert Hormats, chairman of Goldman Sachs International and a former State Department official. If that should happen, the military alliances whose fortunes now seem so bearish could become good investments again.

THE ONE GERMANY[5]

The division of Germany has ended. But the unification of Germany has only just begun. Between October 1989 and October 1990 what once seemed unattainable became a reality: the swift merger of the two Germanys with active support from the

[5]Article by Angela Stent, associate professor of government at Georgetown University, from *Foreign Policy*, 81:53–70 Winter 90/91. Copyright 1991 *Foreign Policy*. Reprinted by permission.

United States and remarkably little resistance from the Soviet Union. German national enthusiasm reached its climax during the first weeks after the opening of the Berlin Wall, as all Germans began to realize the full implications of the collapse of communism. However, by October 3, 1990, the formal reunification date, the harsh economic realities and mounting social costs of the merger were creating a more sober atmosphere across both parts of Germany. As the new German state consolidates itself, many domestic hurdles must be overcome. The way these problems are resolved will fundamentally influence Germany's international role. The Federal Republic of Germany's (FRG) allies—past, present, and future—have begun to see the potential for markedly different relations with the new German state over the next decade.

In 1991, the new Federal Republic must redefine its international role even as it tackles the domestic problems of unification. Germany faces a host of issues: its relationship with its chief ally—until now—the United States; its role in Europe, which will have a major influence on the future of the European Community (EC); and the balance between these old commitments and its expanding ties to the Soviet Union. But the United States and other countries will also help shape Germany's new direction, giving it guidance as it reenters the international community as a fully sovereign member. Questions about Germany's evolving world role abound. Will Germany be willing and able to accept the new political responsibilities that come with economic might? Should Germany's partners encourage Germany to assume a more assertive world role? What stake will the new Germany have in a viable Soviet Union?

Understanding the problems Germany faces in the new decade demands first an examination of the past. Central to a look back is the question of what Germany's division achieved from the perspectives of the main protagonists: the United States, the Soviet Union, and the two German states. The division of Germany represents a classic example of muddling through and improvisation. The United States and the Soviet Union shared one goal in 1945: to prevent Germany from ever again threatening the world militarily. They disagreed, however, on how to achieve this goal.

From the U.S. standpoint, the division of Germany into occupation zones agreed at Yalta and Potsdam was intended as a temporary measure until a more satisfactory solution could be found. No master plan existed for creating a strong West Germany that would eventually become a major strategic asset to America. The deteriorating economic situation in the western zones of Germany, the need for a coherent set of institutions to administer the economy, and the realization that the USSR would not accept this enterprise led to the unification of the American, British, and later French zones. As Soviet policy grew ever more confrontational, the United States became increasingly concerned about preventing further Soviet expansion. Only after the creation of the Federal Republic in 1949 and the consolidation of the U.S. policy of containing the Soviet Union did American views begin to anticipate a future West Germany as a bulwark against Soviet power.

Moscow, like Washington, initially was ambivalent about Germany's future role and had no blueprint. Soviet leader Joseph Stalin expected significant reparations from the western zones of Germany—which he never received—and believed that total Soviet control had to be imposed in his zone to guarantee German loyalty. He feared the establishment of a unified, pro-Western German state; hence his blockade of Berlin in 1948–49. Although Stalin did offer the West a united, neutral Germany in 1952, this proposal sought to prevent West Germany's entry into NATO rather than to create a single state in good faith. Only after Stalin's death did the USSR, like the United States, begin to view "its" Germany as a major political and strategic asset.

Neither the United States nor the Soviet Union, therefore, had a clear idea of what the two German states would become when they were created. Washington believed it was imperative to create a democratic, prosperous West Germany within a democratic Western Europe, ensuring it would remain peaceful; Moscow saw its first priority as taking what was left of East German industry and destroying its remaining democratic political forces. Subjugation would guarantee a compliant Germany. The two German states were objects of U.S., British, French, and Soviet policy rather than active participants in the post-World War II order.

Yet the division of Germany did more to support U.S. strategy in Europe than initially anticipated. Perceptions of Germany changed as the product of both the FRG's rapid development into a democracy with a thriving market economy under Chancellor Konrad Adenauer and the changing international situation. A number of factors altered American perceptions: the founding of NATO in 1949, the outbreak of the Korean war in 1950, the creation of the European Coal and Steel Community in 1951, and then French Foreign Minister Robert Schuman's vision of European unity with a Franco-German axis at its core. Although the United States probably would have accepted German unity if the Soviet Union had agreed to any of the various Western proposals of the 1950s, Washington welcomed the establishment of a strong, pluralistic West German state. By the late 1960s, West Germany had become America's most important NATO partner. The need to guarantee the FRG's security vis-à-vis the Soviet Union became the principal rationale for a continued U.S. military and political presence on the Continent.

For the Soviet Union, the results of Germany's division were more mixed. Unlike U.S. policy toward Germany, which ignored the German Democratic Republic (GDR), Soviet policy was aimed at both Germanys. Moscow actively tried to stabilize the GDR and weaken the FRG's ties with the West.

Until 1961 East Germany took priority. After suppressing the 1953 uprising there, the Kremlin strengthened its commitment to the loyal but unpopular Stalinist Walter Ulbricht. The presence of Soviet troops supported the GDR government as it consolidated control and achieved what was regarded as its own "economic miracle." The construction of the Berlin Wall in 1961 finally stabilized the regime by effectively imprisoning the population. The GDR emerged as the Soviet Union's most important trading partner, and its army as a pillar of the Warsaw Pact. By 1969, East Germany had become a critical security asset for the Kremlin.

Soviet achievements toward the FRG proved rather meager in the 1950s and 1960s. The Kremlin failed to prevent the FRG from joining NATO. West Germany's refusal to recognize East Germany—or indeed any other East European country—along with its close ties to the United States were the major impediments to improved Moscow-Bonn relations. The division of Germany remained a major Soviet objective as long as the FRG remained a revisionist power refusing to recognize the postwar status quo. Ironically, the timing of Nikita Khrushchev's ouster as Soviet leader in October 1964 was dictated by his forthcoming visit to the FRG. He was accused, after his fall, of trying to "sell out" East Germany to West Germany. Said one of his opponents, then Soviet Presidium member Mikhail Suslov, close Soviet-GDR relations "are not for sale, even if all the gold in the world were offered for them."

During this era of reconstruction, the two Germanys developed very different stakes in the division. Amid occupation and the loss of sovereignty, Adenauer's Federal Republic maintained a constitutional commitment to reunification. This commitment, however, could not obscure the fact that West Germany benefited politically and economically from Germany's division. The chancellor himself, a Catholic Rhinelander, showed less interest in unification than in ties with the EC and especially with France. The opposition Social Democrats, initially the party of reunification, changed their position in 1960 as the issue lost domestic poignancy.

The GDR, by contrast, fared much worse from the separation. It lost much of its industry to the Soviet Union during the late Stalin years, and millions of its population fled to West Germany before the completion of the Berlin Wall. Arguably, the small elite around Ulbricht prospered, but the East Germans did significantly less well than their Western cousins. After 1961, East Germans were often said to be living in a "niche" society, making individual peace with their existential predicament. The events of 1989 revealed just how fragile and unsatisfying those niches were.

Détente and the Germanys

Détente changed both inter-German relations and the attitudes of the superpowers toward their respective German allies. New risks were suddenly introduced into the delicate German balance. The division of Germany became less total, the Berlin Wall more porous. The United States and the Soviet Union began to experience new frictions with the two Germanys as the FRG and the GDR normalized diplomatic relations and developed their own inter-German dialogue. Both superpowers and the two German states accepted the status quo of the division of Germany. Yet even though détente initially reinforced the separation of the two states, it ultimately led to unification because it undermined the East German system.

Adenauer was critical of President John Kennedy's tentative moves toward détente with the USSR after the Cuban Missile Crisis of 1962. But a decade later, the tables were reversed. In the 1970s American policymakers were worried that Moscow would play its "German card" and entice the FRG away from NATO with promises of closer inter-German ties. The United States grew uneasy about the pace of then Chancellor Willy Brandt's *Ostpolitik*—his policy of rapprochement with the Soviet Union and Eastern Europe—

and his willingness to question the seriousness of the Soviet threat to West Germany. As U.S.-Soviet détente disintegrated at the end of the 1970s, Washington and Bonn openly disagreed over the state of East-West ties, with the FRG insisting on retaining the fruits of its own détente with the Soviets. The litany of U.S.-West German disputes that ensued—the neutron bomb, the Siberian gas pipeline, the deployment of Pershing and nuclear-armed cruise missiles—highlighted the development of FRG foreign-policy interests that were sometimes opposed by the United States.

Despite these new U.S.-FRG tensions, exacerbated by concerns over West Germany's trade surpluses with America, Washington and Bonn were able to hold on to the core of the relationship. Until shortly after the Wall fell, the United States saw no reason to question the centrality of its alliance with the Federal Republic, which justified and made possible its large, ongoing military presence in Europe.

The Soviet Union, by contrast, found it increasingly difficult to choreograph the triangular relationship between Bonn, East Berlin, and Moscow in the 1970s and 1980s. Ultimately, but too late, the Soviets realized that what had improved its ties to West Germany threatened its interests in East Germany. The Kremlin did not foresee the corrosive effect inter-German rapprochement would have on East German society. Détente between the two Germanys undermined whatever legitimacy the GDR system had by ending its international isolation, increasing contacts between the two populations, and bringing scenes of freedom and prosperity from West German television into East German homes.

The GDR remained an asset to the Soviets in foreign-policy terms until recently through its support of Soviet activities in Africa, the Middle East, and Latin America. East Germany also remained a loyal member of the Soviet bloc. However, as U.S.-Soviet relations hit a low point in the mid-1980s, the thinly disguised polemics between East Berlin and Moscow over the need to maintain inter-German détente signaled the end of GDR compliance. The Soviets finally succeeded in forcing party leader Erich Honecker to cancel a scheduled trip to Bonn in 1984. But after 1985 the GDR became highly critical of changes in Soviet policy, with Honecker reproaching Moscow for straying from the true socialist path.

The GDR continued to be the Soviet Union's leading trading partner and its top supplier of advanced technology. However, the relationship increasingly drained Soviet energy resources as the USSR supplied cheap, soft-currency oil to the GDR and its other East European dependents, thereby forfeiting potential hard currency earnings. By 1985 it was debatable whether the GDR represented a net economic asset to the Soviet Union.

Mikhail Gorbachev already knew that the old-style socialist system was finished when he decided to stop propping up the increasingly vituperative Honecker amid antigovernment protests in 1989. However, until shortly before the first free East German elections in March 1990 the Soviets expected the continuation of two German states, one capitalist and one reformed communist. Gorbachev did not appreciate the extent of the GDR economy's weakness, nor how rapidly the East Germans would demand unification as their only hope for material salvation.

Over the two decades before unification, Soviet ties with the FRG improved but then deteriorated during the latter years of Leonid Brezhnev and the pre-Gorbachev interregnum. Soviet–West German ties ultimately proved more durable than Soviet–East German relations despite Moscow's failure to weaken the Federal Republic's ties with NATO. The economic hopes pinned to enhanced relations with West Germany never materialized because the Germans remained skeptical about potential economic and political payoffs. Nevertheless, when Gorbachev resumed cordial relations with Bonn in 1987, the favorable experience of *Ostpolitik,* as practiced by such German statesmen as Chancellors Willy Brandt and Helmut Schmidt and Foreign Minister Hans-Dietrich Genscher, was able to ensure a receptive response by the West German government and public.

At the beginning, West Germany's détente with the Soviet Union carried no great expectations. Brandt's *Ostpolitik* even reflected a sense of resignation. He accepted the postwar status quo and recognized East Germany. He also realized the revisionist *Ostpolitik* practiced by previous governments had failed to change the status quo. As Brandt explained in his memoirs, *People and Politics: The Years 1960–1975:*

I was well aware that, throughout its phases of historical development, Germany had never entirely corresponded to the "classic nation-state". . . . I nevertheless remained convinced that the nation would live on. . . . Germany had always existed as a cultural nation, and it was as a "cultural nation" that it would retain its identity.

Through its rapprochement with the Soviet Union and Eastern Europe, the FRG rehabilitated itself internationally. West Germany's growing economic and political strength enabled it to play a key role in the Conference on Security and Cooperation in Europe (CSCE) process and to become a major force in East-West relations. *Ostpolitik* ultimately paid off, inasmuch as relations between the two German states radically improved after 1969.

After Brandt's resignation in 1974, the FRG engaged in a constant balancing act between its *West-* and *Ostpolitik*. West Germans depended on the United States for security, but on the Soviet Union for continued inter-German rapprochement. Tense U.S.-Soviet relations presented Bonn with unwelcome choices, though it ultimately accepted the major U.S. policy decisions. Generally content with its role as a major economic and political player in Europe, the FRG wanted no significant responsibilities outside Europe and consigned its ultimate defense to the United States.

Despite official West German commitment to unification and pursuit of closer ties with the GDR, the German political establishment did not believe unification would occur for decades. In 1988 Chancellor Helmut Kohl was asked, "Will you yourself experience unification?" He replied, "No, probably I will not live to see it." Indeed, before the Wall's breakdown—and even for some time afterward—few members of the political establishment seriously desired unification. The inter-German relationship—essentially East German humanitarian concessions in return for West German economic largesse—had seemingly stabilized the GDR and reinforced its separateness. West Germany had achieved an acceptable modus vivendi with the GDR regime that amounted to the management of partition.

In the early détente era, the GDR benefited internationally from the belated diplomatic recognition it secured from the FRG in 1972. East Germany's international stature and activities grew. However, increased international legitimacy did not translate into greater domestic legitimacy. Honecker's policy of *Abgrenzung*—insulating East German society from the pernicious effects of close contact with West Germany—failed miserably. Despite Honecker's increasing contempt for Gorbachev, he understood that Soviet troops were all that stood between the GDR leadership and political oblivion. But even as he grew increasingly out of touch with domestic realities, he must have calculated that the GDR was the linchpin of the Soviet security glacis in Europe. Thus, Honecker must have believed he could blackmail Moscow into preserving his power because without him communism in East Germany would disappear. Such thinking proved to be a fatal miscalculation.

The Soviet Union, facing a domestic economic crisis and widespread ethnic tensions, simply could not afford to underwrite the East German system. The division of Germany for which the Soviet Union had worked so hard no longer enhanced Soviet security. The GDR proved too expensive and rested on shaky political foundations. The 40-year-old edifice of the "first workers' and peasants' state on German soil" crumbled within two months. Its reason for a separate existence extinguished, the GDR quickly became extinct. Thus the Soviet Union ultimately helped create what had always been depicted as its worst postwar nightmare—a united, capitalist Germany in NATO.

The New Nationalism

What direction will German foreign policy take now that Germany is united and sovereign? The Kohl government has reassured the world that unification merely adds 16 million Germans and five new states to the Federal Republic and thus will have a limited impact on future policies. Some, however, both inside and outside Germany, worry aloud that unification will encourage the resurgence of historical ambitions and aggression that were only contained by division. Between these two extremes, some observers argue that Germany can adopt a new, responsible leadership role, though only through considerable effort. The new German challenge comprises four aspects: domestic post-unification developments and their impact on foreign policy; German-Soviet relations; Germany's role in the EC; and German-U.S. relations.

Although the GDR included one-third of pre-war German territory and had only 16 million inhabitants, numbers alone offer a misleading view of unification. The psychological impact of uniting the two Germanys will be considerably greater than statistics suggest. For the first time in 45 years, Germany is not an occupied country and has finally paid for its role in World War II. How will the new German national identity evolve, now that Germany is one again? The evidence from the Federal Republic is encouraging. Citizens there have internalized democratic, nonviolent, even antimilitarist, values. Those who fear a resurgent German militarism should remember that in the first half of the 1980s the United States was primarily concerned with an excess of pacifism and antinuclear sentiment in Germany. If the experience of postwar West Germany is any guide, the new German nationalism will not be aggressive, but rather directed toward peaceful, all-European goals. Certainly, all the treaties signed during unification stress Germany's historical responsibilities and its future peaceful world role.

The East German contribution to the new national identity is less certain. Before 1990 East Germans had an incomplete national consciousness. They never believed in a separate socialist German identity but they were also not West Germans. Instead, their local regions provided their sense of *Heimat,* or homeland. Therefore, East Germans have yet to develop a viable German identity. Moreover, East Germans possess a pronounced inferiority complex vis-à-vis their West German cousins, further complicating the process of integration. The East Germans face the challenge of developing a national identity that will assure they are fully integrated into the new Germany and are not second-class citizens. The overriding goal of the 1989 revolution was to oust the repressive government so the people could lead normal lives. Supporters of the overthrow did not seek to reestablish a mighty German state. Since the liberation from communism, right-wing, antiforeigner, anti-Semitic, and militaristic groups have formed in East Germany as they have in all East European countries; but their numbers remain small and the groups are unlikely to find much support in a united Germany unless a worldwide recession has a major impact on the German economy.

The economic problems of unification complicate the process of political integration. No one knows how much unification will cost; speculation puts the price at far more than anyone had originally envisioned: more than DM 775 billion (more than $500 billion). Unemployment is rising in the eastern part of Germany. The social dislocations are also considerable. Hard questions will persist in both parts of Germany about why unification had to happen so fast and whether it had to be so disruptive. But given Germany's inherent economic strength, it will eventually overcome the current problems and expand its economic influence in both parts of Europe.

The addition of the GDR to the FRG should not, in the near future, have much direct impact on German foreign policy. West German policymakers will continue to make Germany's foreign policy, and East German leaders will have little influence on the new Germany's international posture. Moreover, foreign policy did not occupy an important place in the East German population's political consciousness. GDR foreign policy concentrated on supporting Soviet activities in the Warsaw Pact and the Third

World. These policies tied East Germany to some of the least appealing regimes, and did not represent a major source of pride to East Germans. In fact, most East Germans are generally opposed to an activist German foreign policy, particularly if it involves military force.

Ultimately, the way Germans view their new world role will depend on how they come to terms with the past. The West Germans have, to a large extent, acknowledged and condemned their Nazi past. The acrimonious *Historikerstreit*—the debate in the FRG in 1985–88 over whether, among other things, the enormity of Stalin's crimes somehow diminishes the uniqueness and horror of Nazism—revealed how controversial some questions remain. But at least there has been debate. The East Germans have not fully examined or accepted their past; instead they were taught that West Germany was the sole inheritor of the Nazi state. Indeed, East Germans must grapple with two pasts: Nazi and communist. They must face these legacies simultaneously as they integrate into West Germany. They may be tempted to claim they were victims, placing all the blame on Hitler, Stalin, Ulbricht, and Honecker. But East Germans' refusal to acknowledge shared responsibility for these two dark pasts would not bode well for their future attitudes toward the outside world.

German-Soviet relations will be another key determinant of the new Germany's world view. Traditionally, Russia and Germany have carried on a love-hate relationship. From Peter the Great's invitation to Germans and other Europeans to build up Russia's economy and the nineteenth century rise to political prominence of the Baltic Germans to the Rapallo Treaty of 1922 and the Nazi-Soviet Pact of 1939, Germans and Russians have both admired and feared each other. Their common bonds run deep and, in modern history, periods of amity have outnumbered periods of enmity. Prussians in particular have always believed that their destiny was entwined with Russia's, though Western-oriented Germans like Adenauer and Kohl more often looked across the Rhine rather than the Elbe—until Kohl had the imperative of unification thrust on him. The Cold War therefore represents an aberration rather than the norm in a shared Russo-German destiny.

There are a variety of opinions in the Soviet Union on that country's future relationship with Germany. Some Soviets in recent months have reiterated a traditional theme: A new Rapallo represents the ideal vision of the future, a special Soviet-German

relationship of mutual interest with Germany unfettered by en-
tangling alliances. Key discussions about unification were consciously held in places with historical resonance: Brest (formerly
Brest-Litovsk), Münster, and Moscow itself, where the Treaty on
the Final Settlement with Respect to Germany was initialed in
September 1990. When the Rapallo pact was completed, the Soviets and Germans were international outcasts. The secret military
collaboration that preceded the treaty represented the only way
Germany could rearm. In the 1990s some Soviets might well
dream of a new Rapallo with Germany, but such an agreement
would hold little attraction for the Germans. Germany will have
no interest in exchanging its role in Europe and the Western
alliance for an exclusive pact with the Soviets.

Nonetheless, Germany will play an important role in the Soviet Union's evolution in the foreseeable future. Both countries are
counting on this influence. The USSR would like to restore the
Russo-German economic relationship to its pre-1914 position.
Germany traditionally acted as Russia's most important trading
partner, with bilateral trade being largely complementary. Germany always provided more economically to Russia than vice ver-
sa. In 1913, for instance, 47 per cent of Russian imports were
from Germany while Russian exports to Germany were 29 per
cent of Russian exports. In 1989, the two Germanys together
were the USSR's largest trading partner. In the near term, it is in
Germany's interest to give considerable economic assistance to
Moscow in order to stabilize Gorbachev's beleaguered government and ensure that the 380,000 Soviet troops withdraw from
Germany without incident there or disruption in the USSR. The
FRG has already agreed to pay the Soviets DM 12 billion (about $8
billion) to support, repatriate, and retrain Soviet soldiers. This
sum will grow in the future. In the longer run, through trade and
eventually direct investments, Germany will enlarge its economic
presence in the Soviet Union. Yet Germany cannot save the Soviet
economy; and if the Soviets' ambitious program for a transition to
a market economy fails, all the German capital and expertise in
the world will not be able to keep the Soviet economy afloat
indefinitely.

If the Soviet economy does recover sufficiently, the USSR might
well develop a relationship of economic dependence on Germany.
This arrangement would suit Germany well, provided the FRG
receives economic and perhaps political compensation. The economic payoffs might involve privileged access to Soviet raw mate-

rials. The political payoffs might come through cooperation with the Soviets in a refurbished all-European security arrangement that would remove any future Soviet threat to Germany.

The loss of East Germany might at first seem a damaging blow to Soviet security. But in the long run the USSR may benefit from German unification once it has redefined its security interests. Since the ring of loyal, communist buffer states no longer exists and Germany has no aggressive designs on the Soviet Union, Moscow is beginning to redefine security in terms of a multilateral all-European system. The Soviet Union sees Germany as its entree to Western Europe, both politically and economically. The Soviets hope to collaborate with Germans to institutionalize a security system that will eventually make NATO, like the Warsaw Pact, obsolete, thereby eliminating the growing asymmetry between a moribund Eastern pact and a healthy, though restless, Western alliance.

Germany's relationship with the USSR will also include cooperative arrangements for Eastern Europe. As Moscow struggles to find its way out of communism, it is losing the ability to exercise influence over the countries of its former empire. Indeed, Germany is poised to become the most important power in Eastern Europe. It will most likely be a major force in reconstructing Eastern Europe once the unification process is finished. But stabilizing these countries is also in the Soviet interest. However, what kind of role the USSR will be willing or able to play in Eastern Europe in the future remains unclear.

These scenarios are premised on the continued existence of the Soviet Union. The Germans, like most others outside the Soviet Union, want Gorbachev to remain in power and successfully complete his agenda. To this end, they will do everything possible to support his government. But ethnic, regional, and political fissures are widening within the Soviet Union, and Germans may be faced with a prospect that they fear: serious instability in the western regions of the USSR. Germany could work effectively with a future independent Russian Republic under the leadership of Boris Yeltsin, for example. But Germany would have difficulty coping with demands from ethnic Germans in the Soviet Union or Poland, or indeed with demands from independent Baltic states or the Ukraine if the USSR breaks up. Neither the Germans nor any other major power would welcome a reopening of sensitive questions involving ethnic German minorities and the boundaries of Central Europe.

The New German Identity

Once unification is successfully completed, Germany is poised to become the premier power in Europe—Eastern and Western. However, members of the EC are increasingly concerned that the preoccupation with the unification process and the added burdens of the Soviet Union and Eastern Europe may dilute Germany's enthusiasm for European integration. Until now, Germany has been an engine of integration. Before the revolutions of 1989, the single European market of 1992 was the major West European concern. Now the issue has faded from the public eye, partly because the demise of communism and the return of German unity have gripped attention. But the EC, and Germany's role in that organization, will significantly shape the new German identity. The addition of East Germany complicates the process because East Germans, unlike West Germans, lack a European consciousness. They remain more provincial and unaccustomed to being part of the EC. European integration will receive less domestic support in Germany as a whole until the 16 million eastern Germans develop a European identity. Moreover, some Germans may conclude that the economic and political demands of the EC must take second place to those of unification.

The problems and readjustments of unification may reinforce the sense that momentum toward closer European political union is slowing. The Persian Gulf crisis has revealed the difficulties of achieving political cooperation. It seems certain that during the trying process of unification the FRG cannot help but be less involved in Europe and more self-absorbed; this preoccupation may have a long-term effect on developments within the EC, including questions of expansion with new Central European members. The French and others increasingly ask whether Germany will be willing to quickly renounce its newly regained political and economic sovereignty to a supranational European entity.

Of all the basic factors in Germany's future outlook, the relationship with the United States appears to be the most predictable and the strongest. After all, Germany might not yet have been united had it not been for the Bush administration's immediate and unwavering support for unification and its pressure on the USSR to speed up the process. At the very least, the external aspects of unification would not have been so quickly resolved.

But the past 40 years of strong relations furnish no guarantee of future closeness. Unification may ultimately prove detrimental to U.S. security interests—possibly more detrimental than to Soviet interests—unless policymakers redefine U.S. interests. Both sides must devote hard thought to how their relationship might be restructured. The United States will no longer be the chief guarantor of German security in the post–Cold War, post-unification world. Once Soviet troops withdraw from Germany, pressure will grow in Germany (as well as in Washington) to remove most of the American troops. Moreover, as new security structures evolve in Europe, Germans may increasingly question their membership in NATO, particularly if the Social Democratic party were to enter office again. The psychological impact of unification and the restoration of sovereignty remains unknown. But Germans will inevitably reassess their dependence on the United States, formerly an integral part of Bonn's foreign policy. The United States, for its part, will have to rethink its reasons for stationing troops in Europe if the primary military mission and Soviet threat no longer exist.

Since World War II, U.S.-German ties have developed on a variety of levels and the basis for a continuing partnership will persist. But that geopolitical partnership will not continue unaltered in the new era. Reshaping U.S.-German relations will require a conscious effort. Otherwise, Germans may resent what they view as a continuing unequal relationship, and Americans may see the Germans as ungrateful erstwhile allies who turned their backs after Washington worked hard to ensure German unification. As it did in the immediate postwar situation, the United States knows what it does not want Germany to be but is unsure about what it wants Germany to become.

Perhaps the answer is to redirect the focus away from an exclusive U.S.–German relationship and develop a more multilateral American policy toward Western Europe as a whole. Until now, Washington has perceived its relationship with Germany primarily in bilateral terms. Although it encouraged the founding of the EC, partly as a means of anchoring West Germany peacefully in Europe, it has conceived of the U.S.–FRG relationship as the centerpiece of its European policy. This exclusive focus on Germany might prove harmful to U.S.–German relations in the future if the United States becomes disappointed by the lack of immediate tangible response from the Germans in light of the strong U.S. support for unification.

To avoid this possible disillusionment and its negative repercussions for U.S. policy, Washington should modify its policy of focusing separately on each European country and actively support the FRG's continued role in a more integrated Europe, even if that implies a reduced U.S. role. Moreover, as long as NATO is alive and well—and it may well last into the next century in some form—the United States should encourage the Europeanization of the alliance with a less dominant U.S. role.

In general, the most productive way to assist the transformation of U.S.-German relations is to encourage Germany's active membership in multilateral organizations in which the United States also participates. Indeed, both within and without Germany support remains strong for the concept of channeling German ambitions and energies through broader international frameworks. Kohl and Genscher of late have been stressing Germany's commitment to strengthen the CSCE process—and herein lies an opportunity for Washington. There is considerable skepticism in the United States about the CSCE's effectiveness as a security organization; but many East European countries view the CSCE as the most promising future security institution—short of the entire Warsaw Pact joining NATO. The United States should actively contribute to the reorganization of CSCE, which will ensure an important American role on the continent while it strengthens Germany's commitment to Europe. Other multilateral structures may either be created or redesigned, including a West European defense force; but all should serve to integrate Germany in a series of structures designed to assure Europe's peaceful future.

The most basic question is how the new Germany will adapt to its future leadership role. German ability to exercise appropriate, responsible leadership will depend both on domestic developments and on outside guidance. Germany has become an economic giant, but has consciously limited its own political engagements. With the support of other NATO members, the FRG has hidden behind its constitution to justify its unwillingness to project power overseas militarily or politically in cooperation with its allies. But as Kohl and his colleagues have realized in the Gulf crisis, Germany will now have to reconsider those constitutional provisions that prevent its playing a more assertive international role. As in the case of Japan, it is worth pondering whether it is wise to encourage Germany to become a world power again. No casual decision can be made on such an important subject. But realistically, the FRG will have to assume new responsibilities in a world with a considerably weakened Eastern Europe and Soviet Union.

If the past 40 years are any guide, Germany will be able to develop leadership qualities suitable to itself and its neighbors. Germany is surely capable of playing a constructive international political role commensurate with its economic might. The process of reasserting leadership will not be smooth and will require sensitivity from the Germans and cooperation from old and new allies. If the Federal Republic succeeds in forging this new identity, then the united Germany will become a great power with a major voice in shaping the twenty-first century.

BIBLIOGRAPHY

An asterisk (*) preceding a reference indicates an excerpt from the work has been reprinted in this compilation.

BOOKS AND PAMPHLETS

Allen, Bruce. Germany east: dissent and opposition. Black Rose Books. '89.

Ardegh, John. Germany and the Germans: an anatomy of society today. Harper & Row. '88.

Balfour, Alan. Berlin: the politics of order, 1738–1989. Rizzoli. '90.

Bark, Dennis L. A history of West Germany. Oxford University Press. '89.

Burns, Rob and vander Will, Wilfried. Protest and democracy in West Germany. St. Martin's Press. '88.

Campbell, Edwina S. Germany's past and Europe's future: the challenges of West Germany's foreign policy. Bergamon-Brassey's. '89.

Childs, David. The GDR: Moscow's German ally. Unwin Hyman. '88.

———. et al., eds. East Germany in comparative perspective. Routledge. '89.

Clemens, Clay. Reluctant realists: the Christian democrats and West German Ostpolitik. Duke University Press. '89.

Dalton, Russell J. Politics in West Germany. Scott Foresman. '89.

Dennis, Michael. German Democratic Republic: politics, economics, and society. Pinter. '88.

Fritsch-Bournazel, Renata. Europe and German reunification. Berg. '91.

Goeckel, Robert F. The Lutheran church and the East German state: political conflict and change under Ulbricht and Honnecker. Cornell University Press. '90.

Grass, Gunter. Two states—one nation? Harcourt Brace Jovanovich. '90.

Hancock, M. Donald. West Germany: the politics of democratic corporatism. Chatham House. '89.

Hansieder, Wolfram F. Germany, America, Europe: forty years of German foreign policy. Yale University Press. '89.

Hulsberg, Warner. The German Greens: a social and political profile. Verso. '88.

James, Harold. A German identity: 1770–1990. Routledge. '89.

Katzenstein, Peter J. Industry and politics in West Germany: toward the Third Republic. Cornell University Press. '89.

Koch, Karl, ed. West Germany today. Routledge. '89.

Kolinsky, Eva. The Greens in West Germany: organization and policy making. Oxford University Press. '89.

––––––. Women in West Germany: life, work, and politics. Oxford University Press. '89.

Larrabee, F. Stephen, ed. The two German states and European security. St. Martin's Press. '89.

Leaman, Jeremy. The political system of West Germany, 1945–85: an introduction. St. Martin's Press. '88.

Lipschitz, Leslie and McDonald, Donogh, eds. German unification: economic issues. International Monetary Fund. '90.

Maier, Charles. The unmasterable past: history, holocaust, and German national identity. Harvard University Press. '88.

Marsh, David. The Germans: a people at the crossroads. St. Martin's Press. '90.

Marshall, Barbara. The origins of post-war German politics. Croom Helm. '88.

Mattox, Gale A. and Vaughan, John H. Germany through American eyes: foreign policy and domestic issues. Westview. '89.

Merkel, Peter H. The Federal Republic of Germany at forty. New York University Press. '89.

Munzenberg, K. J., ed. Advances in the Federal Republic of Germany. Lippincott. '90.

Ninkovich, Frank A. Germany and the United States: the transformation of the Germany question since 1945. Twayne. '88.

Ostrow, Robin. Jews in contemporary East Germany. St. Martin's Press. '89.

Paul, Barbara Dotts. The Germans after World War II: an English language bibliography. G. K. Hall. '90.

Peacock, Alan and Willgerodt, Hans, eds. Germany's social market economy: origins and evolution. St. Martin's Press. '89.

Rueschemeyer, Marilyn and Lemke, Christiane. The quality of life in the German Democratic Republic: changes and development in a state socialist society. M. E. Sharpe. '89.

Schwartz, Thomas A. America's Germany: John J. McCloy and the Federal Republic of Germany. Harvard University Press. '91.

Smith, Gordon, et al. eds. Developments in West German politics. Duke University Press. '89.

Sodaro, Michael J. Moscow, Germany, and the West from Khruschev to
    Gorbachev. Cornell University Press. '90.
Steiner, Rolf. The German question. Columbia University Press. '90.
Thomaneck, J. K. A. and Mellis, James. Politics, society, and government
    in the German Democratic Republic: basic documents. Oxford Uni-
    versity Press. '89.
Tietmeyer, Hans and Guth, Wilfried. Two views of German unification.
    Group of Thirty (Washington, D.C.). '90.

ADDITIONAL PERIODICAL ARTICLES WITH ABSTRACTS

For those who wish to read more widely on the subject of the
reunification of Germany, this section contains abstracts of additional articles that bear on the topic. Readers who require a comprehensive list of materials are advised to consult the *Readers'
Guide to Periodical Literature* and other Wilson indexes.

Germany unbound. Timothy Garton Ash. *The New York Review of
Books* 37:11–15 N 22 '90

Although Germany has legally become an all-German state of unity, estimates vary on the number of years it will take before Germany is really
prepared for unification. There will be costs for reconstructing East German industry, and social tensions will arise from that reconstruction. New
Germany will have to prepare a plan for its responsibilities outside Europe and within Europe and will need a new national identity.

German history, more or less as Germans see it. Otto Friedrich.
Smithsonian 21:82–90+ Mr '91

Although many people see Germany as an aggressive nation, German
history before the 20th century was marked by attacks from belligerent
neighbors. In 1618, despite a truce between Catholics and Protestants,
fighting resumed over control of Bohemia, a Germanic principality, and
lasted for 30 years. Known as the Thirty Years' War, this is the most
overwhelming example of a pattern of repeated attacks by foreigners, and
the German people still live with the memory of it. With a history of
fragmented territories and autonomous regional rulers, many Germans
look forward to their country's unification. The history of modern Germany's struggle into nationhood is chronicled.

Ambivalence amid plenty. Howard G. Chua-Eoan. *Time* 136:74–
5 Jl 9 '90

Part of a special section on the reunification of Germany. Only 28,000 Jews now reside in West Germany, and many of them feel ambivalent about their decision to live there. Those who live there do so because of economic opportunities, a feeling of affinity for the culture, or a need to prod the German conscience. Most are originally from the Soviet Union or Eastern Europe and find living conditions within the Federal Republic vastly superior to those of their previous existence. According to Werner Bergmann of the Center for Research into Anti-Semitism, the presence of anti-Semitism in West Germany is comparable to that in other Western European nations. It could increase with unification, however, because antiforeign sentiment has become more visible in East Germany.

Kohl paying a price for unification of Germany. Robin Knight and John Marks. *U.S. News & World Report* 110:47 Je 10 '91

German reunification is taking its toll on Chancellor Helmut Kohl and his ruling Christian Democratic Union. As eastern Germany's economy collapses and as taxes skyrocket in western Germany to cover the costs of reunification, a massive switch of allegiance is under way. In contrast to last December, when the Christian Democrats won 42 percent of the vote in East Germany and the opposition Social Democrats garnered 24 percent, recent polls show that the Christian Democrats would win only 28 percent of the vote today; the Social Democrats would get 38 percent. Under the direction of newly elected Bjorn Engholm, one of Germany's most popular leaders, the Social Democrats are gaining support by playing to the increasing discontent over the pace, cost, and direction of reunification. The party will receive another boost if Foreign Minister Hans-Dietrich Genscher, a Free Democrat and the most popular leader in Germany, renews his party's alliance with the Social Democrats.

The difference Willy Brandt has made. Arthur M. Schlesinger. *The New Leader* 73:2, 11–13 O 29 '90

Many of the great themes of the 20th century are embodied in the life of the German Social Democratic Party's Willy Brandt. His uncompromising belief in political freedom began when he joined the party in 1930, at the age of 17. He was so militant an opponent of the Nazis that he had to depart for Norway once Hitler came to power in 1933; he continued the anti-Nazi fight from Sweden after Hitler invaded Norway. From 1957 to 1966, he was mayor of the western half of divided Berlin. With his support, the SPD affirmed its belief in democracy, the mixed economy, the social market, and the welfare state as a middle ground between communism and unbridled capitalism. He then focused his attention on reducing the tensions of the cold war and ending the division of Europe. His Ostpolitik hastened the demoralization of the Communist empire and invigorated reform within the Soviet Union and Eastern Europe. He recently embraced German unification.

A German winter of discontent? Richard Morais. *Forbes* 147:41 Ja 21 '91.

Faced with rising prices, workers in what was once East Germany are becoming increasingly militant. In the East, prices for food and other staples have risen dramatically since reunification, while workers earn wages and salaries that are considerably lower than those received by workers doing similar jobs in the country's West. Eastern railroad workers have already mounted a two-day strike, and several unions have set deadlines for wage and salary parity. Their strategy could backfire if higher wages scare off Western investment, which East Germany needs if it is to develop. A quick rise in national wage costs could cause inflation and massive unemployment, but a much slower one could cause the country to become crippled by industrial inaction.

A tale of two cities: the government abandons Bonn for Berlin. Mary Nemeth. *Maclean's* 104:82 Jl 1 '91

Germany's Bundestag has voted 336 to 321 in favor of making Berlin the capital of the newly reunified country. According to opinion polls, a slight majority of western Germans had favored keeping Bonn as the capital, while more than 70 percent of eastern Germans wanted Berlin. Bonn advocates cited the prohibitive cost of the move and pointed out the city's proximity to the West, its status as a symbol for efficiency and order, and its standing as the center for a government that built West Germany into Europe's economic powerhouse. They also noted that Berlin held uncomfortable memories of Germany's Nazi past. Those who backed Berlin called it a symbol of the new Europe and a possible key arbiter in the post-cold war order of East-West integration. Over the next 12 years, the German ministries and their leaders will move to Berlin, while the upper house of parliament and many city bureaucrats will remain in Bonn to ease the financial impact on the city.

Eastern Germany starts showing a pulse. Gail E. Schares. *Business Week* 48 Jl 15 '91

After a frustrating and painful transition year since reunification, Germany is experiencing some success in its efforts to rebuild the shattered economy of the east. The decision to move the seat of government from Bonn in the more prosperous west to Berlin in the east was seen by many observers as a sign of the Bundestag's determination to speed the east's turnaround. The east's economy is being aided by $86 billion in government spending in 1991, and private investors are contributing another

$37 billion. Most economists now believe that the east German economy is hitting bottom and is due to pick up speed, if only because it can't go any lower. Services are starting to pick up. For example, new building orders leaped to $172 million in May, a 50 percent increase above the total for April. The recovery of the service sector is offering some jobs to offset the continuing layoffs in heavy industry, and startup companies and privatization are also adding jobs.

Where have the Commies gone? John Elson. *Time* 138:35–6 Jl 8 '91

Once 2.3 million strong and embodying the political, intellectual, military, and bureaucratic elite of the country the Communist Party of what was formerly East Germany has fallen on hard times. Now called the Party of Democratic Socialism, it has only 250,000 adherents, most of them former Communist functionaries who remain loyal despite the current discrimination against those linked to the Communist hierarchy or the Stasi. The former party leadership is in disarray, with roughly half the Politburo's former members under investigation for possible treason, corruption, and abuse of power. Other leading party cadres and most members of the East German diplomatic corps have been forced to find new lines of work. Although the Party of Democratic Socialism is the largest political organization in reunified Germany's five eastern states, it has only 17 votes in the 663-seat Bundestag.

Old Nazis, new Nazis (Stasi). Guy Martin. *Esquire* 115:70–5+ Ja '91

With the reunification of Germany, work has begun to dismantle the East German Ministry for State Security, or Stasi. Run by Politburo member and general Erich Mielke, the Stasi controlled every aspect of East German life. The organization consisted of 86,000 regulars and an estimated 2 million unofficial coworkers, and it had officers in the police, the border guards, and in customs. It also had its own 10,000-man army. The Stasi compiled 2 million personal dossiers on West Germans and enemy intelligence-service operations around the world. In addition, it held files on 6 million East Germans, or about a third of the population. The Committee to Dissolve the National Security has been put together to dismantle the Stasi. The committee's job will be difficult because many Stasi files are not accounted for, and their contents may be used to blackmail citizens. Moreover, many ex-Stasi members are still loyal, and the group's influence remains strong.

Berlin's ode to joy. Priit J. Vesilind. *National Geographic* 177:104–32 Ap '90

The opening of the Berlin Wall in November 1989 signaled the end of the 28-year division of the city of Berlin and the beginning of the end of Communist rule in Eastern Europe. Many East Germans crossed into West Germany for the first time and celebrated their new freedom along West Berlin's extravagant shopping street, the Kurfurstendamm. Now that the celebrating is over, new questions about Germany's fate are arising. Some West Germans fear that an influx of East Germans will increase the numbers of the unemployed, the homeless, and drug addicts. Nevertheless, the Berlin Wall will never again be able to forcefully keep Berliners from traveling freely.

Capitulating to capitalism. John Marks. *U.S. News & World Report* 110:38–9 Ja 14 '91

The Soviet Army in Germany is having trouble adjusting to its change in status. Soldiers are deserting, committing suicide, killing one another, and selling weapons to obtain funds for Western goods. The once mighty Soviet Army, three years before the last of its 360,000 troops and 20,000 dependents are to go home, is surrendering to poverty, despair, and capitalism.

America and her friends. Gerald Frost. *National Review* 43:29–31 My 27 '91

Part of a cover story on the political future of Europe. Future security for Europeans and Americans depends on NATO, the only viable basis for transatlantic cooperation on several issues. In the new world order, America will naturally look to its European partners in the Western alliance, but an increasingly united Europe might be less likely to help the United States than in the past. There has been some question about NATO's usefulness, and German foreign minister Hans-Dietrich Genscher has suggested that European security be based on the 34-nation Conference on Security and Cooperation in Europe. NATO remains vital, however, although changes in it are necessary: It will need some strategy to replace flexible response, it may have to be equipped to handle problems arising from huge shifts of populations, and there will have to be new burden-sharing arrangements to relieve the United States of the economic cost.

Kohl. Bruce W. Nelan. *Time* 137:35 Ja 7 '91

Part of a cover story on Time's Man of the Year. Germany's Chancellor Helmut Kohl is one of four men who surprised the world last year. Kohl overcame all obstacles to create a united Germany. When the Berlin Wall came down in November 1989, Kohl knew instinctively that the East German Communist regime was at an end and that the unification of

Germany and the mending of Europe were within reach. Kohl proved to be an able diplomat in his dealings with the Soviet Union by persuading Soviet president Mikhail Gorbachev to modify his opposition to German unity. Gorbachev agreed that Germany had the right to unify and join NATO. In December's all-German election, Kohl became the chancellor of a reunited Germany. In bringing his country and Western Europe to the aid of Eastern Europe, Kohl is continuing to help Europe mend its divisions.

The character issue. Robert D. Kaplan. *The Atlantic* 265:24+ My '90

The conditions and attitudes that plagued Germany's first three Reichs are not prominent today, and prosperity and democracy militate against their return. Whereas the rise of the First Reich convinced Germans of their country's central place in Europe, its fall after the Thirty Years' War sowed bitterness and national frustration. The Second Reich, characterized by a weak parliament, social immobility, and an overbearing and reactionary military caste, represented the postponement of the democratic and economic development that had occurred in other Western European nations. Its defeat and humiliation in the First World War brought about the Third Reich, which resulted in such complete destruction that most of the German national heritage was extinguished. The current character of West Germany will determine the future shape of a unified Germany, in which nationalism will probably remain a marginal force.

Dirty Germany. Charles Benedict. *Buzzworm* 3:30–5 Mr/Ap '91

Unified Germany has discovered that severe environmental problems have developed during the past 45 years of separation. According to a study prepared for Germany's Green Party by the Institut fur Okologische Wirtschaftsforchung, it will take ten years and cost between $250 billion and $315 billion to correct Germany's solvable environmental problems. The report advocates that as the former East German economy moves into a free-market system, industry and agriculture should be reconstructed with high regard to ecological and environmental preservation. Because East Germany is bankrupt, however, the reconstruction must be financed by West Germany, which seems set on remaking the East in its own image. East Germany's massive garbage and pollution problem is largely the result of former contracts that enabled West Germans to dump their wastes in the East.

Helmut Kohl: the people's chancellor. T. D. Allman. *Reader's Digest* 138:109–13 Ap '91

An article condensed from the December 1990 issue of Vanity Fair. As chancellor of the newly united Germany, Helmut Kohl is one of the most important men in the world. Kohl, who lacks polish, makes mistakes, and is emotional, has often been underestimated, especially when it comes to his drive, instincts, and timing. Kohl rose through the political ranks, becoming head of the Rhineland-Palatinate government, chairman of the Christian Democratic Union, and opposition leader in the Bundestag, the lower chamber of the West German parliament. Finally, in 1983, he became West Germany's chancellor. In that position, he masterfully managed the political unification of Germany, and on December 2, his coalition of political parties achieved victory in the first free elections of a united Germany since 1932. To his countrymen, the chancellor is proof that persistence, goodwill, and hard work can make dreams come true.

Managing for a second miracle. Louis S. Richman. *Fortune* 123:221–2+ Ap 22 '91

Despite the problems that have accompanied German reunification, the industrial system and management style responsible for West Germany's dynamic economy remain valid models for the new democratic governments of Central Europe. West Germany's social market economy is a distinctive blend of capitalism and comprehensive social security. The system, which provides a social safety net as well as an enviable balance between work and leisure, is effective because of the West Germans' orthodox approach to running their economy. The Bundesbank, Europe's most independent and inflation-loathing central bank, tenaciously safeguards the deutsche mark, making it the European Community's most stable currency. West Germany's economic strength lies in its thousands of mid-size companies, which look to export sales to fuel their growth. East German industry will have to develop its own such companies in order to thrive.

To the bitter end. Hans Zimmerman. *New Perspectives Quarterly* 7:56–7 Summ '90

In an article adapted from comments made during a tour of Bitterfeld, East Germany, an East German environmentalist discusses the degradation of the dirtiest city in the world. Once full of life, Bitterfeld is now the scene of environmental ruin. During the 1960s, the government increased the production of Bitterfeld's factories by 300 percent as part of its Socialist Reconstruction process. These factories continue to produce toxic products and byproducts under primitive conditions. Because of the heavily polluted air, most of the children in the area suffer from some type of respiratory illness. Pipes pour untreated wastewater into the River Mulde, and the forest on the river's banks has become so polluted that it will never recover. West Germany has approved $500 million to assist in the cleanup effort, but much more is needed to measure and treat the pollution that plagues East Germany.